What others are saying about
The 52 Series . . .

"Gregg's '52 Series' is both practical and helpful. It's a great resource for Christians of all spiritual levels, but perfect for groups focused on new or growing believers. Gregg's books are thoughtful, practical, and make learning fun."

Mark Batterson, *Author,* The Circle Maker *and* Wild Goose Chase

"Our church has invested lots of time and prayer helping people become devoted followers of Christ. We are not interested in merely providing a nice church experience. We want to see people of all spiritual interest levels move forward and grow in their journey of faith. Gregg's '52 Series' is a catalytic resource that encourages movement toward Christ. You'll benefit working through them on your own, but they're even better when shared with a group."

Greg Hawkins, *Executive Pastor, Willow Creek Community Church; Author of* Move

"Finally, a spiritual growth series that not only helps me grow but is also informative and fun. I love that it's something I look forward to reading, can use it with my small group, and feel comfortable sharing it with my friends who have little (but some) spiritual interest. Gregg's '52 Series' has made spiritual growth accessible to everyone. Well done!"

Doug Fields, *Author,* Purpose Driven Youth Ministry & Refuel

"One of the biggest voids in the church is having quality resources which move a new believer toward spiritual maturity. Gregg Farah has both the burden and knack for filling that gap. This series will deepen you in your walk with Christ."

Dave Stone, *Pastor of Southeast Christian Church*

"Many believers want to grow in their faith, yet seem to get stuck on where to start and how to keep going. Gregg Farah has written a series out of his experiences of mentoring believers that give practical ways to help us grow. There are so many times that one small step opens the door to significant life change. By offering 52 ideas, this series will help you to discover those steps that God best uses as he works in you to grow you. I highly recommend studying this in a small group, because your faith will be strengthened as you see how God works in different ways to grow us."

Tom Holladay, *Teaching Pastor at Saddleback Church; Author of* The Relationship Principles of Jesus

"Gregg Farah's 52 Series takes the busy 'city' place inside of us – that restless part that's landlocked between the skyscrapers of our demanding schedule, unmet expectations and our God issues – and invites us to stop, breathe and best of all, 'look up.'"

Stacey Robbins, *Author*, Finding the Missing Peace: Stories from Hell, Heaven and the Other Side of Texas

"As a teacher, student, and practitioner of the faith, Gregg Farah has developed a very creative and relevant approach to discipleship in the "52 Series." This series is a must for churches with a small group ministry searching for effective curriculum!"

Bil Cornelius, *Pastor of Bay Area Fellowship; Author of* I Dare You to Change *and* Go Big

"I love what Gregg has done with the '52 Series.' It's not easy finding resources that work for new and seasoned believers, but Gregg has done it. Each chapter is short and to the point, so they don't intimidate. But the chapters are clear and filled with enough features that they engage people wherever they're at. Great job, Gregg!"

Josh Griffin, *Saddleback Church Pastor, Author of* 99 Thoughts for Small Group Leaders *and* More Than Dodgeball

"What I enjoy most about Gregg Farah's '52 Series' is that I can give the books to anyone in our church. New Christians get their questions answered, and mature Christians get a refresher course and have a terrific tool to disciple others. Gregg does a masterful job getting people to think and dialogue, apply the Bible to their lives, and have fun in the process."

Beau Adams, *Pastor, Community Bible Church*

"With uncommon skill and heart, Gregg Farah has crafted a resource you'll go to again and again. Not only does *The 52 Series* fill a sparse space in the church resource library, it makes growth and life-change accessible to anyone—anyone! If you're hungry, God's word is the means to your fill, and Gregg serves it up in hearty portions."

Michele Cushatt, *Inspirational speaker at notable venues such as* Women of Faith *and* Compassion International *and contributing author for numerous publications including* MOPS International *and* Today's Christian Woman, *and multiple compilation books including five titles in the* Chicken Soup *series.*

52

Reasons to Believe

Concise Thoughts on the Christian Faith

gregg peter farah

Carpenter's Son Publishing

52 Reasons to Believe: Concise Thoughts on the Christian Faith

Copyright © 2012 by Gregg Peter Farah

No part of this book may be reproduced or transmitted in any form or by any means, electronic or mechanical, including photocopying, recording or by any information storage and retrieval system, without permission in writing from the copyright owner.

Published by Carpenter's Son Publishing, Franklin, Tennessee

Published in association with Larry Carpenter of Christian Book Services, LLC
www.christianbookservices.com

Unless otherwise noted, Scripture references are taken from The Holy Bible: New International Version by Biblica. All other references are taken from The Holy Bible: King James Version, as noted.

Cover and Interior Layout Design by Suzanne Lawing

Edited by Robert Irvin

Printed in the United States of America

978-09849772-4-6

All rights reserved.

Table of Contents

Focuses on 20 characteristics and evidences of the Bible and how each gives us a reason to believe the Bible is true.

The Bible is . . .
1. affirmed
2. recognized
3. proven
4. confirmed
5. discovered
6. plentiful
7. reliable
8. meticulously maintained
9. authoritative
10. consistent
11. surviving
12. influential
13. vulnerable
14. honest
15. demanding
16. historical
17. inclusive
18. scrutinized
19. simple and clear
20. life-changing

SECTION 2: God is . . . 101

Reveals 12 descriptions of God, each reminding us of who God is and why we can believe he is with us.

God is . . .
21. more than you can imagine
22. triune
23. near
24. far
25. good
26. powerful
27. all-knowing
28. listening
29. a refuge
30. approachable
31. our friend
32. jealous

SECTION 3: Jesus is . . . 151

Identifies 13 characteristics of Jesus, stating who Jesus is and why we can confidently cling to him.

Jesus is . . .
33. God
34. man
35. forgiving
36. demanding (no hypocrites)
37. understanding (been tempted)
38. the only way to God
39. resurrected
40. our sacrifice
41. a demonstration of God's love
42. committed to us
43. a ransom for many
44. life-changing
45. approachable

Shares seven traits of the Holy Spirit and how each gives us more reasons to believe.

The Holy Spirit . . .

*To Elaine, Rachael, and Kaitlyn. If I could choose
any three girls in the world to be my daughters,
I would pick you. Every single time.*

*May you know Jesus' love in a powerful way, and may
you enjoy an infinite number of reasons to believe.
I love you and am proud of you.*

*Special thanks to the following friends
for giving this project life:*

Janine Farah, Kristin & Ryan Flea-Ficker, Grant &
Bethany Norvell, James & Holly Nobles, Glenn & Cindy
Hall, Max & Caleb Hall, Team Novacheck, the Dantona
Family, the Linsky Family, AWD, David & Glenn Paris,
Ben & Olivia Ward, Brandon & Sheila Williams, Charles
& Julia Chu, Stacey & Rocky Robbins, Kevin & Ginnette
Young, and Chris & Roey Diefendorf.

Thank you everyone for praying for and supporting me
during my writing and indiegogo campaign.

Thank you Bob Irvin for your care, wisdom,
and skill in editing.

Introduction: The Importance of This Book

A forwarded email reminded me, "God wants spiritual fruit, not religious nuts." So true. The evening news and TV sitcoms offer more than enough nuts. Plenty of people talk a good game when it comes to religion, but we want more. We're looking for a healthy, active faith that shows and tells the love of Christ.

I've talked to many people who bemoan their lack of faith and wished they had more biblical knowledge. Nineteenth-century preacher Charles Spurgeon offers hope: "A little faith will bring your soul to heaven. A great faith will bring heaven to your soul."[1] Faith is important, regardless of size. But there is much to gain in building and strengthening faith.

A strong faith . . .
- stands the tests of time
- overcomes
- supports
- encourages
- serves

. . . and *52 Reasons to Believe* will help you get there.

There are many views of the Bible and even more views on God. And because belief on these two subjects — God and the Bible — is so significant, this book offers not one but *52 Reasons to Believe*.

How to Use This Book

A good book can be used many ways. You might choose to read this book on your own, working through a chapter a day or several a week. But I encourage you to grab some friends and coffee and interact with the material together. If you discuss with a group, consider the following plan:

1) Pick one topic (the Bible, God, Jesus, or the Holy Spirit) to focus your study.

2) Read and discuss the material together, one chapter a week . . . or, my suggestion, read the chapter on your own, highlighting sections that made you think, encouraged you, or raised questions. Then use those highlights as the basis for a discussion.

*Want **more ideas** on how to use this book with groups or as a class? See page 225 for numerous ways to do this, including sample studies and a lesson template.*

No matter how you use this series, dig in! Confront your questions, disarm your doubt, and strengthen your spiritual life. This book won't provide all the answers, but it will give you concise thoughts on the Christian faith and *52 Reasons to Believe*.

Enjoy!

Each chapter includes
Reason to believe
Key Quote
Did You Know . . .
Link to Your Life
Small group Discussion
Key Verse
Prayer

SECTION 1: The Bible is . . .

One
The Bible Is . . . AFFIRMED

Ever doubt the Bible to be true? If so you're not alone. I've been there, and plenty of others have, too. I've wrestled, questioned, and challenged the Bible. And it has always won. One observation I've always loved is that Jesus didn't doubt the Bible. His use of the Old Testament (i.e., the Hebrew Bible, the only "Bible" available to him) is significant.

Jesus affirmed it to be true by quoting it

When Jesus was tempted by Satan, the one and only weapon he used was the Word of God (Matthew 4:4, 7, 10). "For the Scriptures say . . . " was Jesus' sword and shield.

Jesus affirmed it to be true by teaching from it

When Jesus met the two men on the road to Emmaus, Luke writes that "Jesus took them through the writings of Moses and all the prophets . . . " (Luke 24:27), a reference that includes the totality of the Old Testament.

Jesus affirmed it to be true by illustrating from it

Jesus tells the story of the rich man and Lazarus. Lazarus begs Abraham for a miracle so his family can believe. Abraham makes it clear that because they have the Bible, they have all they need (Luke 16:19-31).

Jesus affirmed it to be true by basing his purpose on it

In possibly one of the strongest examples of how Jesus viewed the Bible, Matthew 5:17 reveals that Jesus' purpose on earth was to complete the works of Moses and the prophets.

Jesus affirmed it to be true by submitting to it

Despite Jesus' power and authority, his words in Matthew 26:53-54 reveal his willingness to submit to his Father's plan as prophesied in the Scriptures.

Jesus affirmed it to be true by believing all of it

It's tempting to pick and choose what we believe about the Bible; we usually do this based on what we deem credible or possible. Jesus challenges that notion by referencing some of the more "unbelievable" portions of the Bible. In Matthew 12:40, Jesus refers to Jonah and the great fish; in Matthew 24:38, Jesus mentions Noah and the ark; and in Luke 17:32, Jesus describes Lot's wife turning to stone.

KEY QUOTE

"To doubt Christ's teachings is to doubt all that is precious and basic in the Christian faith. Jesus believed the Old Testament and taught its truth. That alone should be enough."[2] — Robert Harris

DID YOU KNOW (DYK)...

"In the King James Version, the four Gospels include 3,779 verses. According to Graham Scroggie, 1,934 of these verses, in whole or in part, contain the words of Christ. Out of these 1,934 verses about 180, or almost one out of ten, cite or allude to the Old Testament. Even this does not give us the full picture, for as John W. Wenham notes, 'In many passages there is simply no way to distinguish between Jesus' conscious allusion to the Old Testament and His normal, habitual use of Old Testament words and thought forms. The Holy Scriptures penetrated the warp and woof of Christ's mind.'"[3]

LINK TO YOUR LIFE

What could you do without today? A car? A home? A dream? There are many things we could go without for a period of time, and the same is true with Jesus. He went without food for 40 days, friends during his greatest need, and glory while on earth. But one thing He always had was a firm conviction in the authority of the Bible.

It was His food, His friend, and His glory. His use of and view of the Bible challenges me. I want to know and lean on the Bible with the same kind of conviction.

SMALL GROUP DISCUSSION

Which of Jesus' affirmations resonates with you most? Are there any you have difficulty accepting? Discuss why you think this is or is not important.

KEY VERSE

"Do not think that I have come to abolish the Law or the Prophets; I have not come to abolish them but to fulfill them. For truly I tell you, until heaven and earth disappear, not the smallest letter, not the least stroke of a pen, will by any means disappear from the Law until everything is accomplished" (Matthew 5:17, 18).

PRAYER

"Father, thank you for Jesus' example. Help me overcome any unbelief I have regarding the authority of your Word. Help me to know, love, and lean on the Bible as Jesus did.

Continue your prayer:

Amen."

Two
The Bible Is . . . RECOGNIZED

A Google search on how to recognize something to be true produces the following articles:

- How to recognize a true friend.
- Ten ways to recognize true love.
- How to recognize true labor.
- How to recognize a true spiritual path.

It also provides a link for a Snoop Dogg video.

But maybe we can go a little deeper than just those references. (I'm guessing we can do better than the Snoop video.)

A Bible search on how Jesus' followers viewed the Bible identifies, among many others, some key verses: 2 Timothy 3:16, 17 and 2 Peter 1:20, 21. In these verses, Jesus' followers recognize the Bible to be true, and in them they write of the authority, scope, and power of the Scriptures.

Both the apostles Paul and Peter give authority to God. "All Scripture is inspired by God," Paul wrote in Second Timothy. And, "the prophets were moved by the Holy Spirit, and they spoke from God," Peter wrote in his second letter in the Bible. If there's any doubt as to what Bible verses come from God, both authors indicate ALL of them do. And Paul offers four valuable uses of the Bible in the Timothy passage: it teaches, rebukes, corrects, and trains.

Jesus' followers had a high view of the Bible's teachings and placed all bets on its truth and ability to change to lives. This is a direct result of Jesus' promises in John 14:25, 26 and John 16:13 that the Holy Spirit would teach them and help them remember all that Jesus said.

KEY QUOTE

"Now if Jesus, who was God in the flesh and always spoke the truth, said that the Old Testament was the Word of God and that the New Testament would be written by His apostles and prophets as the sole authorized agents for His message, then our entire Bible is proven to be from God. We have it on the best of authority — Jesus Christ Himself."[4] — Norman Geisler

DYK . . .

It's one thing to believe the Old Testament to be true based on Jesus' view of it, but Peter identified Paul's teachings to be equally authoritative. In 2 Peter 3:16 he refers to Paul's writings as "Scripture," the same word used 51 times in the New Testament, each referring to the Old Testament.

LINK TO YOUR LIFE

Have you ever doubted what's in the Bible, or whether or not it's true? That's reasonable, particularly when there are many diverse opinions on the subject. But it's worth considering how Jesus' followers viewed the Bible. Sure, they wrote it, but they also risked their lives for the truth within it. Historical documents and legend strongly tell us that Peter died, upside down, while crucified on a cross; Paul was beheaded for his faith; Peter's brother, Andrew, was crucified on an X-like cross; Thomas run through, impaled, in

India, where he went to preach the gospel. The list goes on and on. It's one thing to stake your reputation on whether or not a movie or restaurant is good, but it's quite another to put your life on the line. Jesus' followers recognized the Bible to be true, boldly proclaimed it, and lived according to it.

SMALL GROUP DISCUSSION

How would you respond if someone asked you if the Bible is true? Would anything from this chapter help you respond? Do you disagree with or question anything from this chapter?

KEY VERSE

"Study this Book of Instruction continually. Meditate on it day and night so you will be sure to obey everything written in it. Only then will you prosper and succeed in all you do" (Joshua 1:8, NLT).

PRAYER

"Dear God, it's clear that the New Testament writers had no doubt that their words were from you. Help me to cling to you and your word as they did.

Continue your prayer:

Amen."

Three
The Bible Is ... PROVEN

If you're going to be a good skeptic, you've got to have two words at your disposal: *prove it*. This power duo demands action and places the responsibility of proof on whoever is making a claim. I like the *prove it* phrase. It's fair, it's concise, and it's informative. Anybody can make a claim. But only the proven can back it up.

In the Old Testament period, it wasn't unusual for people to identify themselves as prophets. God had his own version of *prove it* — and the stakes were your life.

> *"But a prophet who presumes to speak in my name anything I have not commanded, or a prophet who speaks in the name of other gods, is to be put to death. You may say to yourselves, 'How can we know when a message has not been spoken by the Lord?' If what a prophet proclaims in the name of the Lord does not take place or come true, that is a message the Lord has not spoken. That prophet has spoken presumptuously, so do not be alarmed"* (Deuteronomy 18:20-22).

The "your life for your word" strategy effectively quieted the false prophets, but it did nothing to squelch the true prophets. The Bible is filled with more than 300 references to a coming Messiah, and all of these prophecies were fulfilled in Jesus Christ. This has caused many skeptics to think twice. Here are just some of these prophecies:

- *"The kings of the earth rise up and the rulers band together against the Lord and against his anointed"* (Psalms 2:2).
- *"Even my close friend, someone I trusted, one who shared my bread, has turned against me"* (Psalms 41:9).
- *"Strike the shepherd, and the sheep will be scattered"* (Zechariah 13:7).
- *"I told them, 'If you think it best, give me my pay; but if not, keep it.' So they paid me thirty pieces of silver. And the Lord said to me, 'Throw it to the potter' — the handsome price at which they valued me! So I took the thirty pieces of silver and threw them to the potter at the house of the Lord"* (Zechariah 11:12, 13).
- *"They will strike Israel's ruler on the cheek with a rod"* (Micah 5:1).
- *"I offered my back to those who beat me, my cheeks to those who pulled out my beard; I did not hide my face from mocking and spitting"* (Isaiah 50:6).
- *"They pierce my hands and my feet"* (Psalm 22:16).
- *"My God, my God, why have you forsaken me?"* (Psalm 22:1).

All of the above Bible verses are taken from the Old Testament, of which Dr. James Kennedy states: the Old Testament "was completed some 400 years before Jesus was born. No critic, no atheist, no agnostic has ever once claimed that any one of those writings was written after His birth. In fact, they were translated from Hebrew into Greek in Alexandria some 150 years before He was born. If this [the Bible] is merely a book written by men, would you please explain to me how these words were written?"[5]

You want proof the Bible is true? Fulfilled prophecy provides it.

KEY QUOTE

"Skeptical minds seek explanations for this phenomenon [fulfilled prophecy]. No satisfactory answer can be given apart from belief that Bible prophecy is a message from God, giving not merely impressions and feelings but definite information and revelations from above."[6] — Robert Harris

DYK . . .

There are 61 major prophecies concerning the life of Jesus Christ, written many hundreds of years before His birth. Even unbelieving scientists applying the measurement of statistical probability tell us that the chance of just eight of those prophecies being fulfilled is one to the 1,017th power (one hundred thousand trillion). This wasn't luck.[7]

LINK TO YOUR LIFE

Not only are fulfilled prophecies bricks that help form a foundation for our faith in the Bible, they serve as evangelistic tools. Let fulfilled prophecies be the seeds to start a conversation about who God is and about the Bible's reliability.

SMALL GROUP DISCUSSION

Explain why you do or don't think the Bible has proven itself to be true. What encourages you or confuses you from this chapter?

KEY VERSE

"Therefore the Lord himself will give you a sign: The virgin will conceive and give birth to a son, and will call him Immanuel" (Isaiah 7:14).

PRAYER

"God, thank you for providing literally centuries of evidence for the authority of the Bible. Give me not only a better understanding of these prophecies but also confidence that your word is true and trustworthy.

Continue your prayer:

Amen."

Four
The Bible Is . . . CONFIRMED

Major League Baseball pitching scouts travel the world to find potential pitching prospects that they can develop into World Series champions. But in 1947, the archaeological world found a young man whose pitching arm made one of the most valuable discoveries in history.

Mohammed Ahmed el-Hamed (called edh-Dhib, or "the Wolf"), a bedouin of the Ta-amireh tribe, was looking for a lost goat. While searching, he tossed a rock into a cave and heard the sound of breaking pottery. He entered and found a broken jar in the midst of dozens of other jars containing parchments wrapped in linen cloth, two of which held the complete Isaiah text. Professor Eleazar Sukenik of the Hebrew University purchased some of the scrolls and wrote in his diary, "It may be that this is one of the greatest finds ever made in Palestine, a find we never so much as hoped for." Dr. W.F. Albright, a world-renowned biblical archaeologist, described the find as "the greatest manuscript discovery of modern times. And there can happily not be the slightest doubt in the world about the genuineness of the manuscript."[8]

So what's the big deal?

The Bible is often criticized as unreliable because it is assumed the text has been edited over the years, despite the claims of biblical scholars that this is not the case. Ancient scribes were meticulous in their craft (discussed further in chapter 8), adhering to strict guidelines. The Dead Sea Scrolls' discovery provided eyewitness proof that the Bible had indeed been copied accurately. The scrolls allowed us to view a document a thousand years older than any we previously had access to. Dr. Gleason Archer explains the significance:

> Even though the two copies of Isaiah discovered in Qumran Cave 1 near the Dead Sea in 1947 were a thousand years earlier than the oldest dated manuscript previously known (AD 980), they proved to be word-for-word identical with our standard Hebrew Bible in more than 95 percent of the text. The five percent of variation consisted chiefly of obvious slips of the pen and variations in spelling. Even those Dead Sea fragments of Deuteronomy and Samuel which point to a different manuscript family from that which underlies our received Hebrew text do not indicate any differences in doctrine or teaching. They do not affect the message of revelation in the slightest.[9]

The Dead Sea Scrolls' discovery confirms that the Bible is accurate, and we can be confident the Bible we read today is consistent with the one originally written.

KEY QUOTE

"About 175 of the 500 Dead Sea Scrolls are biblical. There are several copies of many of the books of the Old Testament, and all the Old Testament books are represented among the scrolls, except Esther."[10] — Charles Ryrie

DYK...

The concentration of salt in the Dead Sea is 10 times higher than that of any other sea or lake on earth. Every liter of its sea water contains an average of 30 grams of salts and other minerals. It is one of the greatest sources of salt in the world.

No animal or plant can exist here. Few fish are found in it, although it is not true that birds that venture near its vapors drop dead.

Because of its high specific gravity, no one will ever sink or drown while bathing there. Nobody has ever committed suicide there by drowning. It was said that Vespasian, commander of the Roman legion which later destroyed Jerusalem in 70 AD, heard of this fact. He tested it by ordering slaves to be thrown into the sea waves with their hands and feet tied. The slaves floated.[11]

LINK TO YOUR LIFE

Your Bible may have been published this year or anytime within the last 20 years. But the text it contains is thousands of years old. And the text you're reading in your Bible today is the same text that Moses and David and Esther and Jesus and the Apostle Paul read. God has spoken, and His message is available to you today.

SMALL GROUP DISCUSSION

Are archaeological discoveries important? On a scale of 1-10 (10 being MOST important), how important is archaeology in affirming the Bible to be true?

KEY VERSE

"Your laws please me; they give me wise advice" (Psalm 119:24, NLT).

PRAYER

"God, it would be easy to doubt your word, but it wouldn't be smart. Your word never fails. Help me love and respect your word more and more each day.

Continue your prayer:

Amen."

Five
The Bible Is . . . DISCOVERED

People of faith don't need to run from archaeology; it's actually a friend to the faith. For years, the Bible's critics have mocked its contents as places that didn't exist, people who never lived, and politics that were never practiced. Some archaeologists, attempting to defend the Bible, have mistakenly claimed to have found "the flood (the great flood of Noah)," the ark of the covenant, the location of the Garden of Eden, and others. Not very helpful. Although well-meaning, contrived efforts aren't necessary. The Bible doesn't need help.

But archaeology does offer much in our understanding of the Bible's contents, along with corroborating its historical truth. But first, it's important to understand the role of archaeology. Walter Kaiser provides great insight:

> The real role of archaeology is not to "prove" the Bible, for that kind of "proof" is available only in certain deductive sciences such as mathematics and logic. On the contrary, the role of archaeology is: (1) to supply cultural, epigraphic, and artifactual materials that provide the background for accurately

interpreting the Bible, (2) to anchor the events of the biblical text in the history and geography of the times, and (3) to build confidence in the revelation of God where the truths of Scripture impinge on historical events.[12]

Kaiser and others have documented the enormous archaeological discoveries made over the last century that strengthen the case for biblical reliability. The apparent missing people, places, and things have been found. And they've been found in abundance.

Author James MacDonald documents three examples.

1) The Ebla Tablets

Bible scholars have often been criticized for claiming that Moses wrote the Pentateuch (the first five books of the Bible). Pundits declared this foolishness! Formal writing didn't exist in 1400 BC, nor did the priesthood or sacrificial system that Moses described. "Then in 1975 the Ebla Tablets were discovered, nearly 20,000 written records dating 1,000 years before the time of Moses. When they were translated, archaeologists found that many of the laws, customs, and sacrificial systems existed long before the time of Moses. Some of the laws and punishments for certain crimes in Scripture actually paralleled the legal thinking of that day."[13] Perhaps Moses knew what he was talking about after all.

2) The Hittites

Despite the Bible's approximate 50 claims of the existence of the Hittites, many university history professors got uptight. There had been no record validating such a people group. They believed this group was a biblical fabrication. However, "recent archaeological digs have found hundreds of references to the Hittite people. They lived over a 1,200-year period in the Middle East."[14] Perhaps some essays will need to be re-graded.

3) Family idols

Genesis 31 tells the story of Jacob, Rachel, and Laban. Rachel stole her father Laban's family idols, or household gods. After three days, Laban realized the idols were missing, and taking many relatives with him, he pursued Jacob and Rachel for seven days. Many have ridiculed this story, wondering why Laban would care so much about items that could be easily replaced. James MacDonald explains: "In 1925 more than 1,000 clay tablets were found at a site in Mesopotamia called Nuzi. These tablets revealed that a person who possessed the family idols could make a legal claim to all of the family property. In other words, as long as Jacob and Rachel had those statues in their hands, they owned everything that was Laban's."[15] Suddenly, the immediacy of Laban's actions make sense.

Archaeology is the Bible's friend.

KEY QUOTE

"There can be no doubt that archaeology has confirmed the substantial historicity of the Old Testament. The excessive skepticism shown toward the Bible by important historical schools of the eighteenth and nineteenth centuries . . . has been progressively discredited. Discovery after discovery has established the accuracy of innumerable details, and has brought increased recognition to the value of the Bible as a source of history." — William Albright,[16] recognized as the preeminent archaeologist of the 20th century day

DYK . . .

The word archaeology is composed of two Greek words: *archaios*, meaning "old" or "ancient"; and *logos*, signifying "word, treatise, or study." A literal definition is "the study of antiquity."[17]

LINK TO YOUR LIFE

Does archaeology prove the Bible to be true? That depends on how you define "prove." It cannot prove who God is or what God has done. But it can prove the historical accuracy of what the Bible states. Millar Burrows sums this up nicely: "Archaeology can tell us a great deal about the topography of a military campaign. It can tell us nothing about the nature of God."[18]

Only the Bible can reveal the true character of God. But this week, you can open your Bible with confidence, knowing that time and time and time and time again, there are archaeological discoveries authenticating the historicity of the Bible. If you want to know God, open your Bible. If you want confidence that the events of the Bible are true, remember what noted archaeologist Nelson Glueck said: "No archeological discovery has ever controverted a single biblical reference. Scores of archeological findings have been made which confirm in clear outline or exact detail historical statements in the Bible."[19]

SMALL GROUP DISCUSSION

Do archaeological discoveries make any impact on your view of the Bible? Explain why or why not. Discuss the Nelson Glueck quote above. Does it alter your view of the Bible in any way? Explain.

KEY VERSE

"Open my eyes to see the wonderful truths in your instructions" (Psalm 119:18).

PRAYER

"God, thank you that I can open my Bible with confidence that it is indeed your word. Help me to hear from you today, that I might live my life in a way that glorifies you.

Continue your prayer:

Amen."

Six
The Bible Is . . . PLENTIFUL

Modern communication is blistering and bountiful. Between blogs, texts, and tweets, words travel fast. That hasn't always been the case. And when speaking about the Bible, that's a good thing. Transmitting the Bible can now be done via email or downloading a document from a website. Long before electricity and printing presses, however, each page of the Bible was copied by hand, a painstakingly long process. We will discuss the process more in a later chapter, but the key in this chapter is the *number* of copies made.

Libraries are filled with classical literature, including works by Homer, Plato, and Aristotle. And it is assumed that the text from these documents are the actual words the authors wrote. *But how do we know?* One of the key evaluative tests historians employ is the bibliographic test, which tests the reliability of the document. It focuses on two key areas:

1) the time span between when the document was written and the earliest copy we have
2) the number of copies available

It is ideal to have a short time span with lots of copies. Homer's

Iliad is considered a highly reliable historical document. There are 643 copies available with a 400-year time gap. The time gap represents the date of the copy compared to when the original was actually written. The *Illiad* is a prize when compared to other historical documents. For example, no one doubts the text of Julius Caesar's *Gallic Wars*, yet we only have 10 copies of that document and the earliest copy was made 1,000 years after the original.

How do these two documents compare to the New Testament? Not very well. While the *Illiad* boasts of 643 copies, there are 5,686 Greek (the language in which it was written) manuscripts of the New Testament. According to the normal means of evaluating historical documents, the New Testament is incredibly reliable.

Further, the time gap for the New Testament is equally astonishing, particularly when compared to other respected historical works. While the *Illiad* has an impressive 400- year gap between copies and the original, the New Testament (NT) can be numbered anywhere between 50 and 225 years. We have fragments of the NT that are believed to be about 50 years from the date of authorship. We have complete NT books 100 years from authorship. Most of the NT can be measured at 150 years, and for a complete NT, the gap is only 225 years.

The biblical evidence supporting its historicity is plentiful. We can read our Bible knowing we are reading the very words of God, as spoken through Jesus, Peter, the Apostle Paul, Moses, David, and many, many others.

KEY QUOTE

"In real terms, the New Testament is easily the best-attested ancient writing in terms of the sheer number of documents, the time span between the events and the document, and the variety of documents available to sustain or contradict it. There is nothing in ancient manuscript evidence to match such textual availability and integrity."[20] — Ravi Zacharias

DYK . . .

The 5,686 New Testament manuscripts represent only those written in Greek. If you added the number written in other languages (like Latin, for example) the total would be 24,970. Even skeptical historians agree that the New Testament is a remarkable historical document.

LINK TO YOUR LIFE

The original Seven Wonders of the World lists sites identified by ancient Greeks as the most notable landmarks in the world. The Bible is so impressive that one writer put together a list of the Seven Wonders of the Word:

1. The wonder of its formation — the way in which it grew is one of the mysteries of time.
2. The wonder of its unification — a library of 66 books, yet one book.
3. The wonder of its age — most ancient of all books.
4. The wonder of its sale — best-seller of all time and of any other book.
5. The wonder of its interest — the only book in the world read by all classes of people.
6. The wonder of its language — written largely by uneducated men, yet the best book from a literary standpoint.
7. The wonder of its preservation — the most hated of all books, yet it continues to exist.[21]

SMALL GROUP DISCUSSION

What is your favorite piece of literature? Have you ever doubted the legitimacy of its authorship? Explain. In what way does this chapter influence whether you do or don't believe the Bible to be true?

KEY VERSE

"Your word is a lamp to guide my feet and a light for my path" (Psalm 119:105, NLT).

PRAYER

"God, your preservation of the biblical text is truly amazing. Help me to read the Bible with the confidence that it is actually your word.

Continue your prayer:

Amen."

Seven
The Bible Is . . . RELIABLE

There is no need to doubt the validity of the Bible. When using the same tests historians use to evaluate other historical works, the Bible passes with high marks. Author Josh McDowell describes his quest to disprove the Bible: "After trying to shatter the historicity and validity of the Scripture, I came to the conclusion that it is historically trustworthy. If one discards the Bible as being unreliable, then one must discard almost all literature of antiquity."[22]

The Bible is reliable. The previous chapter addressed the evaluation of its manuscripts. This chapter will look at two other tests used to determine historical reliability: the internal evidence test and the external evidence test.

Internal Evidence of the Reliability of the New Testament

Internal evidence looks at the authorship of the documents and asks, "How credible are these writings?" There are two ways to do this. The first is to evaluate the consistency of a text — i.e., does it contradict itself? A second is to determine the relationship the authors have with their subjects — i.e., are they writing as eyewitnesses?

Many believe the Bible is filled with contradictions. The Gleason

Archer quote later in this chapter addresses this, but we can agree, for the moment, to say there is a difference between contradictions and apparent contradictions. Often the discrepancy is the result of a failure to apply basic principles of interpretation. Further study of the words, culture, and geography of the Bible reveal there are no contradictions in the Bible.

The writers of the New Testament wrote as eyewitnesses or from firsthand information:

> *"For we did not follow cleverly devised stories when we told you about the coming of our Lord Jesus Christ in power, but we were eyewitnesses of his majesty"* (2 Peter 1:16).

> *"We proclaim to you what we have seen and heard, so that you also may have fellowship with us. And our fellowship is with the Father and with his Son, Jesus Christ"* (1 John 1:3).

External Evidence of the Reliability of the New Testament

External evidence compares other disciplines to either confirm or deny the authenticity and reliability of the document in question. You could be talking archaeology, extra-biblical sources, or secular writers. In other words, how credible are these writings? Are non-biblical writers saying the same thing as what the Bible teaches?

Yes! There are a number of religious and secular historians, archaeologists, and writers who confirm the Bible's authenticity. In Dr. R. Harris' book *Exploring the Basics of the Bible*, he provides several quotes from church fathers:

- **Clement**, Bishop of Rome, wrote that the apostles Peter and Paul preached the Gospel of Christ and were confirmed in the Word with full assurance of the Holy Spirit. He argued that they had perfect foreknowledge of church affairs.
- **Ignatius of Antioch** wrote seven short letters to different

churches and individuals. In his letter to the Ephesians, he referred to "Paul the holy, the martyred, the deservedly most happy," who had written them a letter as well. To the Romans he wrote, "I do not as Peter and Paul issue commandments unto you. They were apostles; I am but a condemned man."

- **Polycarp**, in his youth, knew the apostle John. He referred to the apostles as parallel to the Old Testament prophets. He declared that he could not "come up to the wisdom of the blessed and glorified Paul." In one of Polycarp's letters, he quoted from about half of the New Testament books.[23]

The Bible is reliable. Dr. Clark Pinnock states:

> There exists no document from the ancient world witnessed by so excellent a set of textual and historical testimonies and offering so superb an array of historical data on which an intelligent decision may be made. An honest person cannot dismiss a source of this kind. Skepticism regarding the historical credentials of Christianity is based upon an irrational bias.[24]

KEY QUOTE

"As I have dealt with one apparent discrepancy after another and have studied the alleged contradictions between the biblical record and the evidence of linguistics, archaeology, or science, my confidence in the trustworthiness of Scripture has been repeatedly verified and strengthened by the discovery that almost every problem in Scripture that has ever been discovered by man, from ancient times until now, has been dealt with in a completely satisfactory manner by the biblical text itself — or else by objective archaeological information.

The deductions that may be validly drawn from ancient Egyptian, Sumerian, or Akkadian documents all harmonize with the biblical record; and no properly trained evangelical scholar has anything to fear from the hostile arguments and challenges of humanistic rationalists or detractors of any and every persuasion. There is a good and sufficient answer in Scripture itself to refute every charge that has ever been leveled against it. But this is only to be expected from the kind of book the Bible asserts itself to be, the inscripturation of the infallible, inerrant Word of the Living God."[25] — Gleason Archer

DYK...

The first division of the Bible into chapters and verses is attributed to Stephen Langton, Archbishop of Canterbury — in the late 12th century.[26]

LINK TO YOUR LIFE

Are friends, family members, or classmates claiming that the Bible is full of errors and contradictions? Ask them to provide specific examples and help them research them one by one. It's always good to try to discern whether the individuals making these claims have specific, genuine, intellectual questions they're wrestling with, or shallow, insincere clichés revealing an anti-supernatural bias.

SMALL GROUP DISCUSSION

Share your view of the Bible. Have you always felt this way or has your view changed over time?

KEY VERSE

"Your laws are perfect and completely trustworthy" (Psalm 119:138, NLT).

PRAYER

"Heavenly Father, again and again you provide support for the reliability of your Bible. Give me excitement and confidence to open the Bible and hear from you.

Continue your prayer:

Amen."

Eight

The Bible Is ... METICULOUSLY MAINTAINED

Norman Geisler writes that the Bible is the most accurately transmitted book from the ancient world. No other ancient book has as many, as early, or more accurately copied manuscripts.[27] Rabbi Aquiba (from the 2nd century, AD) is credited with stating that the accurate transmission of the text (the Hebrew Scripture, or Old Testament) is a fence, meaning all kinds of standardized processes were formed in order to fence out any error.

Numerous scholarly groups have been selected over the ages to ensure manuscript purity. Here's an example of one group, the Talmudists, who served from the years 100-500 AD. Samuel Davidson identifies the intricate system they employed so the rolls would be copied meticulously.

[1] A synagogue roll must be written on the skins of clean animals,

[2] prepared for the particular use of the synagogue by a Jew.

[3] These must be fastened together with strings taken from clean animals.

[4] Every skin must contain a certain number of columns, equal throughout the entire codex.

[5] The length of each column must not extend over less than 48 nor more than 60 lines; and the breadth must consist of thirty letters.

[6] The whole copy must be first-lined; and if three words should be written without a line, it is worthless.

[7] The ink should be black, neither red, green, nor any other color, and be prepared according to a definite recipe.

[8] An authentic copy must be the exemplar, from which the transcriber ought not in the least deviate.

[9] No word or letter, not even a *yod*, must be written from memory, the scribe not having looked at the codex before him . . .

[10] Between every consonant the space of a hair or thread must intervene;

[11] between every new parashah, or section, the breadth of nine consonants;

[12] between every book, three lines.

[13] The fifth book of Moses must terminate exactly with a line; but the rest need not do so.

[14] Besides this, the copyist must sit in full Jewish dress,

[15] wash his whole body,

[16] not begin to write the name of God with a pen newly dipped in ink,

[17] and should a king address him while writing that name he must take no notice of him.[28]

Davidson's research adds that any copies that were not made according to the above regulations were either buried or burned. The Talmudists were so convinced of their work that their duplicates would be given equal authority with previously confirmed manuscripts.

Was their work effective? When two copies of the book of Isaiah were discovered as part of the Dead Sea Scrolls collection near the Dead Sea in 1947, they were a thousand years earlier than the oldest dated manuscript previously known (980 AD). Josh McDowell wrote in his excellent book, *Evidence for Christianity*: "They proved to be word-for-word identical with our standard Hebrew Bible in more than 95 percent of the text. The 5 percent of variation consisted chiefly of obvious slips of the pen and variations in spelling. They do not affect the message of revelation in the slightest."[28] Impressive! We can be certain we are reading God's Word as intended because of the meticulously maintained transmission process.

KEY QUOTE

"It may safely be said that no other work of antiquity has been so accurately transmitted."[30] — William Green

DYK . . .

The scribes who were commissioned to make copies of the Old Testament text were required to perform a religious ceremony each time the name of God was written.

LINK TO YOUR LIFE

Are there prized possessions in your life that you look after with the utmost care? Today's security measures include computer firewalls, external hard drives, safety deposit boxes, and Fort Knox. All are designed to give us peace of mind that our belongings are safe. I am humbled (and thankful!) for the care that ancient scribes took to protect God's word from corruption. I often look at the Bible as just any old book when, in reality, it is a prized possession that I ought to cherish.

SMALL GROUP DISCUSSION

Were you surprised by anything in this chapter? What are your thoughts about the Rabbi Aquiba statement at the beginning of this chapter?

KEY VERSE

"The Lord watches over you — the Lord is your shade at your right hand; the sun will not harm you by day, nor the moon by night" (Psalm 121:5-6).

PRAYER

"God, again and again you provide ample evidence to trust that the Bible I read today includes the very words you want me to read. Thank you for your faithful followers who preserved the Bible. May I read it with joy and confidence.

Continue your prayer:

Amen."

Nine

The Bible Is . . . AUTHORITATIVE

Most Christians believe the Bible is an authoritative book, but on what grounds? Scholars and Bible teachers can offer opinions, but what does the Bible say about itself? The Bible definitively claims that its words are inspired by God and, therefore, authoritative. Yet, as Wayne Grudem asks, "But in exactly what sense does the Bible claim to be our authority? And how do we become persuaded that the claims of Scripture to be God's Word are true?"[31]

Much of this book addresses these questions on varying levels. But, using text from Norman Geisler's *A General Introduction to the Bible*, let's evaluate how the Bible claims that its very words are indeed God-given:

1. It is the claim of the classical text that the *writings* are inspired (2 Timothy 3:16, 2 Peter 1:20, 21).
2. It is the emphatic testimony of Paul that he spoke in *"words . . . taught by the Spirit"* (1 Corinthians 2:13).
3. It is evident from the repeated formula "It is *written*" (Matthew 4:4, 7, 10).
4. Jesus said that the words *written* *i*n the entirety of the Old Testament spoke of Him (Luke 24:27, 44; John 5:39; Hebrews 10:7).

5. The New Testament constantly equates the Word of God with the *Scripture (writings)* of the Old Testament (Matthew 21:42; Romans 15:4; 2 Peter 3:16).
6. Jesus indicated that not even the smallest part of a *Hebrew word* or *letter* could be broken (Matthew 5:18).
7. The New Testament refers to the *written* record as the "oracles of God" (Hebrews 5:12).
8. Occasionally the writers were even told to "not omit a *word*" (Jeremiah 26:2), and John even pronounced a curse upon all who would add to or subtract from the "*words* of the book of this prophecy" (Rev. 22:18, 19).
9. The very *words* uttered by men in the Old Testament were considered to be God's words by the New Testament writers. It may be an academic option to deny that the Bible claims "verbal inspiration" for itself, but it is clearly not a biblical possibility.[32]

Not only does the Bible claim itself to be authoritative, Jesus does as well. He does so both through his words and actions. In describing the Bible, Jesus says that it is truth (John 17:17), and when tempted by the devil, He combats the devil with Scripture: "It is written . . . " (Matthew 4:4, 7, 10). Good news: if you read your Bible, you're reading the authoritative Word of God.

KEY QUOTE

"How then does a Christian, or anyone else, choose among the various claims for absolute authorities? Ultimately the truthfulness of the Bible will commend itself as being far more persuasive than other religious books (such as the Book of Mormon or the Qur'an), or than any other intellectual constructions of the human mind (such as logic, human reason, sense experience, scientific methodology, etc.). It will be more persuasive because in the actual experience of life, all of these other candidates for ultimate authority are seen to be inconsistent or to have shortcomings that disqualify them, while the Bible will be seen to be fully in accord with all that we know about the world around us, about ourselves, and about God."[33] — Wayne Grudem

DYK . . .

Early church leader Tertullian devoted his days and nights to Bible reading, so much so that he learned much of it by heart, even its punctuations.

Theodosius the Younger could repeat any part of the Scripture exactly and discourse with the bishops at court as if he himself were a bishop.

Another early church father, Origen, never went to meals or to sleep without having some portions of the Scriptures read.

French theologian Theodore Beza could repeat all of Paul's epistles in Greek at age 80.

Cramer could repeat the entire New Testament from memory, learning it on his journey to Rome.

Ridley also memorized the entire New Testament during his walks in the Pembroke Hall of Cambridge.[34]

LINK TO YOUR LIFE

Psalm 119 is a terrific passage to read to gain a greater love for God's Word. Two of my favorite verses in Psalm 119 are verses 18 and 60.

- *"Open my eyes to see the wonderful truths in your instructions"* (Psalm 119:18, NLT).
- *"I will hurry, without delay, to obey your commands"* (Psalm 119:60, NLT).

I use the first verse as a prayer before I open my Bible. Too often I'm thinking about all I will accomplish *after* reading the Bible, instead of ignoring everything else so that I can focus on what God wants to say to me through the Bible. The second verse inspires me to live for and love God with abandon. I love the enthusiasm and love for God the psalmist shares in that verse.

SMALL GROUP DISCUSSION

Which of the nine Bible claims above surprise you or encourage you? What response do you have to the actions by the historical figures in the DYK . . . section?

KEY VERSE

"Make them holy by your truth; teach them your word, which is truth" (John 17:17, NLT).

PRAYER

"God, your Word is amazing. May it be the final authority in my life.

Continue your prayer:

Amen."

Ten
The Bible Is . . . CONSISTENT

There's a lot to be said for consistency. A consistent employee, athlete, or product is reliable. You know what you're getting because of a proven track record. Consistency breeds confidence. Fortunately, the Bible's message is incredibly consistent, despite its varied background.

Josh McDowell, in *Evidence for Christianity*, summarizes the Bible's unique resume, claiming it to be the only book that was . . .

1. Written over about a 1,500-year span.
2. Written by more than 40 authors from every walk of life, including kings, military leaders, peasants, philosophers, fishermen, tax collectors, poets, musicians, statesmen, scholars, and shepherds.
3. Written in different places: the wilderness, in a dungeon, in a palace, inside prison walls, and many other locations.
4. Written at different times: in times of war and sacrifice as well as of peace and prosperity.
5. Written during different moods: the heights of joy, the depths of sorrow and despair, during times of certainty and conviction, and in days of confusion and doubt.
6. Written on three continents: Asia, Africa, and Europe.

7. Written in three languages: Hebrew, Aramaic, and Greek.

8. Written in a wide variety of literary styles, including poetry, historical narrative, song, romance, didactic treatise, personal correspondence, memoirs, satire, biography, autobiography, law, prophecy, parable, and allegory.

9. The Bible addresses hundreds of controversial subjects — subjects that create opposing opinions when mentioned or discussed. The biblical writers treated hundreds of hot topics — marriage, divorce and remarriage, homosexuality, adultery, obedience to authority, truth-telling and lying, character development, parenting, the nature and revelation of God — among them. Yet from Genesis through Revelation, these writers addressed them with an amazing degree of harmony.

10. In spite of its diversity, the Bible presents a single unfolding story: God's redemption of human beings. The unifying thread is salvation from sin and condemnation to a life of complete transformation and unending bliss in the presence of the one merciful and holy God.

11. Finally, and most important, among all the people described in the Bible, the leading character throughout is the one, true, living God made known through Jesus Christ.[35]

KEY QUOTE

"The Bible is a *biblos*, a single book. It has two Testaments, better called covenants or agreements between God and His people. Those two parts of the Bible are inseparably related: the New Testament is in the Old concealed, and the Old is in the New revealed.

"They form a meaningful and purposeful whole, as they convey the progressive unfolding of the theme of the Bible in the person of Christ. The law gives the foundation for Christ, history shows the *preparation* for Him. In poetry there is an *aspiration* for Christ and in prophecy an *expectation* of Him. The Gospels of the New

Testament record the historical *manifestation* of Christ, the Acts relate the propagation of Christ, the Epistles give the *interpretation* of Him, and in Revelation is found the *consummation* of all things in Christ."[36] — Norman Geisler & Wiliam Nix

DYK...

"Contrast the books of the Bible with the compilation of Western classics called the *Great Books of the Western World*. The Great Books contain selections from more than 450 works by close to 100 authors spanning a period of about twenty-five centuries: Homer, Plato, Aristotle, Plotinus, Augustine, Aquinas, Dante, Hobbes, Spinoza, Calvin, Rousseau, Shakespeare, Hume, Kant, Darwin, Tolstoy, Whitehead, and Joyce, to name but a handful. While these individuals are all part of the Western tradition of ideas, they often display an incredible diversity of views on just about every subject. And while their views share some commonalities, they also display numerous conflicting and contradictory positions and perspectives. In fact, they frequently go out of their way to critique and refute key ideas proposed by their predecessors.

"The uniqueness of the Bible as shown above [the 11 characteristics] does not prove that it is inspired. It does, however, challenge any person sincerely seeking truth to consider seriously its unique quality in terms of its continuity."[37]

LINK TO YOUR LIFE

The Bible's consistency challenges my own spiritual life. I long to be consistent in all I say, think, and do, yet often fall short. The Bible's one consistent message, despite the book's incredible diversity, reveals the priority of Jesus. I want Jesus to be more of a priority in my life . . . starting now.

SMALL GROUP DISCUSSION

Does the Bible's consistency make a difference to you? Explain. What stands out to you from this chapter?

KEY VERSE

"Tune your ears to the world of Wisdom; set your heart on a life of Understanding. That's right — if you make Insight your priority, and won't take no for an answer, Searching for it like a prospector panning for gold, like an adventurer on a treasure hunt, Believe me, before you know it Fear-of-God will be yours; you'll have come upon the Knowledge of God" (Proverbs 2:2-5, The Message).

PRAYER

"God, the Bible makes it clear that you have one message for me: to know Jesus Christ and follow him in everything. Help me make that my priority today.

Continue your prayer:

Amen."

Eleven
The Bible Is ... SURVIVING

As a pastor, I interact with people's questions about God and the Bible all the time. Often, people are apologetic about their questions, as if they're insulting God for not knowing more. I make it a point to encourage people to not only ask their questions but also to have the freedom to ask more. God is not intimidated or angered by our questions. In the same way, the criticism the Bible has received over the years has not caused it to bend or break. The Bible has *survived*.

The Bible has survived the test of time. Historically speaking, the printing press is relatively new. Prior to its advent, the Bible's text had to be copied and recopied by hand on perishable materials. Previous chapters of this book document the success of handmade copies; the Bible's survival over thousands of years before printing presses is clearly miraculous.

The Bible has survived persecution. Historical accounts reveal numerous attempts by individuals or governments to burn or ban the Bible. When the Jews were attacked by Antiochus Epiphanes in the second century B.C., all copies of the Pentateuch (the first five books of the Bible) were burned and anyone found possessing a copy was condemned to death. And despite the changing political climate in recent years, many nations still ban the Bible or the practice of Christianity. For more information, visit websites like www.persecution.com and www.visionbeyondborders.org.

The Bible has survived criticism. In his book *Protestant Christian Evidences*, Bernard Ramm writes, "No other book has been so chopped, knived, sifted, scrutinized, and vilified. What book on philosophy or religion or psychology or belles lettres of classical or modern times has been subject to such a mass attack as the Bible? With such venom and skepticism, with such thoroughness and erudition? Upon chapter, line, and tenet? A thousand times over, the death knell of the Bible has been sounded, the funeral procession formed, the inscriptions cut on the tombstone, and the committal read. But somehow the corpse never stays put."[38] Atheist Thomas Paine committed to destroying the Bible to such an extent that, he said, not even five copies would exist. Centuries later, many homes hold more than five copies themselves.

Despite the numerous challenges, God's Word continues to flourish and can be found all over the world in numerous languages. The Bible is going nowhere. It is a survivor.

KEY QUOTE

"The rain and snow come down from the heavens
and stay on the ground to water the earth.
They cause the grain to grow,
producing seed for the farmer
and bread for the hungry.
It is the same with my word.
I send it out, and it always produces fruit.
It will accomplish all I want it to,
and it will prosper everywhere I send it" (Isaiah 55:10, 11, NLT).

DYK...

Voltaire, the noted French infidel who died in 1778, said that in 100 years from his time Christianity would be swept from existence and passed into history. But what has happened? Voltaire has passed into history, while the circulation of the Bible continues to increase in almost all parts of the world, carrying blessing wherever it goes.[39]

Oh yes, another item of interest: 50 years after Voltaire's death, his home and personal printing press were used to produce Bibles.

LINK TO YOUR LIFE

If God's Word is not going anywhere, it behooves us to take it seriously. What goal(s) can you set to insure you know it and live it? Is there a verse you can memorize? A book you can read? Have you read through the gospels? The New Testament? The Old Testament? The entire Bible?

My family and I are going to begin memorizing a series of verses together. Set a goal and start working toward it today.

SMALL GROUP DISCUSSION

Who is someone (from any historical period) that you would describe as a survivor? Is the Bible's survival record important to you in any way? Explain.

KEY VERSE

"Heaven and earth will pass away, but my words will never pass away." — Jesus (Mark 13:31)

PRAYER

"God, your Word is amazing. Thank you for its stability and power. May it change my life.

Continue your prayer:

Amen."

Twelve
The Bible Is . . . INFLUENTIAL

I read a story in which the author described his first trip to a former Communist country after the Berlin Wall came down. His publishing company brought dozens of cases of Bibles to be distributed at a trade show. When the doors opened, nearly all exhibits were ignored except for the one offering the free Bibles. They quickly disappeared, much to the disappointment of the hundreds who remained, begging for a copy. One man, the author describes, stood out. He was an older man, likely in his 70s, who stood beside the empty display, pointing at the pile of empty boxes stacked up behind the table. Unable to understand the man's language, the author asked an interpreter to explain that there were no more Bibles available. The interpreter talked with the man and then shared with the author, "He would like simply to have a box that carried the Word of God."

It can be easy to lose sight of the power and influence of the Bible when it is so readily available. Another author tells the story of a man in a small village in Poland who received a Bible from a traveler. Years later, the traveler returned and sought to find the man. He did and was pleased to discover that not only had the man become a follower of Jesus, but his entire family had as well, along with many from the village. They gathered to worship, and the traveler was astonished at how much Scripture the villagers had committed to memory. It turned out that, collectively, 200 of the villagers had the entire Bible memorized amongst themselves. About a dozen memorized the entire gospels of Matthew and Luke. Another knew the entire book of Psalms. When the Bible was shown to the traveler, its pages were hardly legible because it had become so worn with use. The words of President Theodore Roosevelt came to mind: "A thorough knowledge of the Bible is worth more than a college education."[40]

Norman Geisler writes, "No book has been more widely disseminated and has more broadly influenced the course of world events than the Bible. The Bible has been translated into more languages, been published in more copies, influenced more thought, inspired more art, and motivated more discoveries than any other book in history."[41] Indeed, billions of copies of the Bible have been published, making it the all-time bestseller. No book comes close to that kind of impact.

Susan Gallagher and Roger Lundin offered this assessment, "The Bible is one of the most important documents in the history of civilization, not only because of its status as holy inspired Scripture, but also because of its pervasive influence on Western thought. As the predominant world view for at least fourteen centuries, Christianity and its great central text played a major role in the formation of Western culture. Consequently, many literary texts, even those in our post-Christian era, frequently draw on the Bible and the Christian tradition."[42]

I've got good news. The world's most influential book is available for you to read, and its author is God. He's got some life-changing things to share. Interested?

KEY QUOTE

"An inspired work, the Bible is also a source of inspiration. Its impact has no equal, whether on the social and ethical plane

or on that of literary creation. We forget too often that the Bible pertains equally to the artistic domain. Its characters are dramatic, their dramas timeless, their triumphs and defeats overwhelming. Each cry touches us, each call penetrates us. Texts of another age, the biblical poems are themselves ageless. They call out to us collectively and individually, across and beyond the centuries."[43]
— Elie Wiesel, renowned novelist and Nobel Peace Prize recipient

DYK...
A microfilm packet containing Genesis 1:1 in 16 languages and a complete RSV Bible were deposited on the moon by Apollo 14 lunar module commander Edgar Mitchell.[44]

LINK TO YOUR LIFE
This is not a guilt trip but hopefully a wake-up call: Keep track of the amount of time you invest consuming information. Whether it's news via the web, TV, or radio, tabulate how much time you listened or watched. Do the same for entertainment, whether movies enjoyed at a theater at home, or TV shows watched by yourself or with friends. Don't forget to include the time spent listening to music.

Now track the same amount of time you spent reading and reflecting on the Bible. If you're like me, that exercise is humbling. And it's not meant to force-feed more Bible into your life. Instead, it's important to evaluate what kind of influence we truly give the Bible in our lives. Now I hope you do stay culturally informed, enjoy your favorite TV shows, and sing your heart out to your favorite songs. But also take time to allow the God of the universe to invade your brain and soul. In fact, let the Bible serve as the filter for all you watch, read, and listen to.

SMALL GROUP DISCUSSION
Who or what are the current top influences in your life? Has that changed in the last five to 10 years? Explain.

KEY VERSE

"How sweet are your words to my taste, sweeter than honey to my mouth!" (Psalm 119:103)

PRAYER

"God, we live in an age that worships celebrities yet ignores your Word. Forgive me for the times I've pushed the Bible aside. Give me an increasing understanding of the power and influence of the Bible, and I pray that it would influence me. Change me, God, through the power of your word.

Continue your prayer:

Amen."

Thirteen
The Bible Is . . . VULNERABLE

Several years ago, Norman Geisler and Frank Turek wrote the excellent book, *I Don't Have Enough Faith to Be an Atheist*. In it, they charge that based on the abundance of material in support of an accurate Bible and a risen Savior, it takes more faith to not believe in Christ than it does to believe. It's an interesting premise, and the book is a worthwhile read.

One of the points the authors make regarding the veracity of the Bible is that it has to be true because of its vulnerability. If the Bible is nothing more than a made-up story, then it would make sense to make the Bible's characters heroes who are courageous and faithful, right? That's certainly not the case in the Bible. Instead, Geisler and Turek refer to "the principle of embarrassment" test that historians use in determining whether or not an author is telling the truth. "Since most people do not like to record negative information about themselves, any testimony that makes the author look bad is probably true."[45]

Does the Bible contain any information that makes the authors look bad? Listen to this assessment from Geisler and Turek: "The people who wrote down much of the New Testament are characters (or friends of characters) in the story, and often they depict themselves as complete morons:

- They are dim-witted — numerous times they fail to understand what Jesus is saying (Mark 9:32; Luke 18:34; John 12:16).
- They are uncaring — twice they fall asleep when Jesus asks them to pray (Mark 14:32-41). They make no effort to give their friend a proper burial, but record that Jesus was buried by Joseph of Arimathea, a member of the Jewish Sanhedrin — the very court that had sentenced Jesus to die.
- They are rebuked — Peter is called "Satan" by Jesus (Mark 8:33), and Paul rebukes Peter for being wrong about a theological issue. Paul writes, "When Peter came to Antioch, I opposed him to his face, because he was clearly in the wrong" (Galatians 2:11). Now keep in mind that Peter is one of the pillars of the early church, and here's Paul including in Scripture that he was wrong!
- They are cowards — all the disciples but one hide when Jesus goes to the cross. Peter even denies him three times after explicitly promising, "I will never disown you" (Matthew 26:33-35). Meanwhile, as the men are hiding for fear of the Jews, the brave women stand by Jesus and are the first to discover the empty tomb.
- They are doubters — Despite being taught several times that Jesus would rise from the dead (John 2:18-22; 3:14-18; Matthew 12:39-41; 17:9, 22, 23), the disciples are doubtful when they hear of his resurrection. Some are even doubtful after they see him risen (Matthew 28:17)!"[46]

The Bible's authors had their chance to pad their resumes. They didn't. Instead they told the truth. And because of that, we think of doubting Thomas, fear-filled Peter, adulterous David, and on and on. The Bible's authors reveal the truth about themselves because they found truth in Jesus. Their honesty gives their stories credibility — and gives us another reason to trust the Bible.

KEY QUOTE

"Why would the apostles lie? . . . If they lied, what was their motive, what did they get out of it? What they got out of it was misunderstanding, rejection, persecution, torture, and martyrdom. Hardly a list of perks!"[47] — Peter Kreeft

DYK . . .

It's true. The apostles were normal humans called to do extraordinary things. And along the way, their humanity was revealed. And even though we got to see them "in process," Jesus changed their lives in ways that are beyond question. We can take solace when we read of their foibles, but let's not forget the power of transformed lives. The apostles died in peace, but they did not die without pain. According to tradition:

- Matthew suffered martyrdom by being slain with a sword at a distant city in Ethiopia.
- Mark expired at Alexandria, after being cruelly dragged through the streets of that city.
- Luke was hanged upon an olive tree in the classic land of Greece.
- John was put in a cauldron of boiling oil, but escaped death in a miraculous manner, and was afterward banished to Patmos.
- Peter was crucified at Rome with his head downward.
- James the Greater was beheaded at Jerusalem.
- James the Less was thrown from a lofty pinnacle of the temple and then beaten to death with a fuller's club.
- Bartholomew was flayed — his skin stripped from his body — alive.
- Andrew was bound to a cross, where he preached to his persecutors until he died.
- Thomas was run through the body with a lance at Coromandel in the East Indies.
- Jude was shot to death with arrows.
- Matthais was first stoned and then beheaded.

- Barnabas of the Gentiles was stoned to death at Salonica.
- Paul, after various tortures and persecutions, was at length beheaded in Rome by the Emperor Nero.[48]

LINK TO YOUR LIFE

Ever feel like you don't measure up? You're in good company. The Bible is filled with fallen people whom God used in extraordinary ways. Take some time today to make a list of all the reasons God might not choose to use you. When you're done, pray and ask God to use you despite your faults or poor choices. Then rip up the paper and throw it away, thanking God that His power is greater than any weakness. Feels pretty good, doesn't it? Go God!

SMALL GROUP DISCUSSION

How did this chapter resonate with you? Explain. What's something that you agreed with, disagreed with, or wanted to learn more about?

KEY VERSE

"Brothers and sisters, I do not consider myself yet to have taken hold of it. But one thing I do: Forgetting what is behind and straining toward what is ahead, I press on toward the goal to win the prize for which God has called me heavenward in Christ Jesus" (Philippians 3:13-14).

PRAYER

"God, thank you for using average people to do extraordinary things. I'm inspired by the heroes of the Bible, but it's nice to know they were human, too. Help me live a faith-filled life for you.

Continue your prayer:

Amen."

Fourteen
The Bible Is . . . HONEST

Some call them spin doctors; others call them liars. Whether you have something to gain or lose will certainly color your word choice. Stated positively, the term *spin doctor* describes public relations experts whose job is to put a positive "spin" on an event or situation. Think Enron, BP Oil, the American Red Cross, entertainment maven Paris Hilton, or baseball player Barry Bonds, and you've got context for companies and individuals who have sought the services of PR firms.

What does this have to do with our view of the Bible? Everything. The writers of the New Testament were not only honest about themselves, describing their foolish behavior and sometimes false beliefs, but they were blatantly honest about their leader, Jesus. If the goal of the writers was to prove that Jesus was the sinless God-man, they would have been wise to leave out some seemingly embarrassing details of His life. For example, Jesus:

- is considered "out of his mind" by his mother and brothers (his own family), who come to seize him in order to take him home (Mark 3:21, 31)
- is not believed by his own brothers (John 7:5)
- is thought to be a deceiver (John 7:12)

- is deserted by many of his followers (John 6:66)
- turns off "Jews who had believed in him" (John 8:30, 31) to the point that they want to stone him (John 8:59)
- is called a "drunkard" (Matthew 11:19)
- is called "demon-possessed" (Mark 3:22; John 7:20, 8:48)
- is called a "madman" (John 10:20)
- has his feet wiped with the hair of a prostitute (an event that had the potential to be perceived as a sexual advance — Luke 7:36-39)
- is crucified by the Jews and Romans, despite the fact that "anyone who is hung on a tree is under God's curse" (Deuteronomy 21:23; Galatians 3:13)[49]

This is not the most flattering depiction of Jesus. Norm Geisler continues: "Nor are these qualities congruent with the Jewish expectation that the Messiah would come to free them from political oppression. In fact, according to their own Bible at the time (the Old Testament), Jesus was cursed by God for being hanged on a tree! The best explanation for these embarrassing details is that they actually occurred, and the New Testament writers are telling the truth."[50]

Geisler and Frank Turek's book also provides a number of Jesus' "hard sayings" that New Testament writers would have ignored if they were making up a story about Jesus being God. Some examples:

- Jesus declares, "The Father is greater than I" (John 14:28).
- Jesus seems to predict, incorrectly, that he's coming back to earth within a generation (Matthew 24:34).
- Jesus then says about his second coming that no one knows the time, "not even the angels in heaven, nor the Son" (Matthew 24:36).
- Jesus seems to deny his deity by asking the rich young ruler, "Why do you call me good? . . . No one is good — except God alone" (Luke 18:19).

- Jesus is seen cursing a fig tree for not having figs when it wasn't even the season for figs (Matthew 21:18).
- Jesus seems unable to do miracles in his hometown, except to heal a few sick people (Mark 6:5).[51]

While there are reasonable explanations for all the difficult statements, it does not make sense for the writers to claim Jesus as the God-man when He's depicted as a sacrificial lamb. Why not just put a cape on Jesus and let Him fly? Because regardless of the counsel modern PR firms would provide, the writers presented Jesus exactly as He appeared. They told the truth.

KEY QUOTE

"The Bible is not an end in itself. The Bible is not a destination; it's a bridge to a better place. That place is a personal relationship with Jesus Christ. We don't worship a book; we worship the One who wrote the book."[52] — James MacDonald

DYK...

While the Bible is the Word of God and, as such, cannot have any errors, nonetheless, this does not mean there are no *difficulties* in it. However, as St. Augustine wisely noted, "If we are perplexed by any apparent contradiction in Scripture, it is not allowable to say, the author of this book is mistaken; but either the manuscript is faulty, or the translation is wrong, or you have not understood."[53] In other words, the mistakes are not God's goofs, but man's misinterpretation. The Bible doesn't make mistakes, but critics do. Critics' accusations of error in the Bible are the result of some error of their own.

LINK TO YOUR LIFE

Jesus and the Bible writers didn't pretend to be someone they weren't. They told the truth even when it could affect their reputations. This week, be honest with God, yourself, and others.

Take a risk to reveal the real you. There may be consequences, but you'll lay a foundation of truth that blesses you and honors God.

SMALL GROUP DISCUSSION

Do you find any of the descriptions of Jesus embarrassing? Why or why not? How valuable is it to you that the Bible is honest about itself and its characters? Why does it or does it not make a difference to you?

KEY VERSE

"Then you will know the truth, and the truth will set you free" (John 8:32).

PRAYER

"Heavenly Father, you are truth. Help me to live a life of truth. Empower me to speak honestly, even when it's difficult.

Continue your prayer:

Amen."

Fifteen

The Bible Is . . . DEMANDING

There are many reasons to believe the Bible is true and comes directly from God. Of all of them, this one — for me — is the most logical. Marketing 101 acknowledges that its goal is to make selling nonessential. In other words, give the people what they want. *In Principles of Marketing*, Philip Kotler writes, "If the marketer does a good job of identifying consumer needs, developing appropriate products, and pricing, distributing, and promoting them effectively, these goods will sell very easily."[54]

The Bible's writers would not have passed Marketing 101. If anything, they provided plenty of illustrations of what not to do. Instead of downplaying the cost of commitment as a nonissue, Jesus does the opposite. He raises the bar with some demanding standards. Norm Geisler illustrates this using Jesus' Sermon on the Mount.

Excerpts from The Sermon on the Mount	Undesirable implications of these commands
"I tell you that anyone who looks at a woman lustfully has already committed adultery with her in his heart" (Matthew 5:28).	If thinking about a sin is sinful, then everyone—including the New Testament writers—is guilty.

Excerpts from The Sermon on the Mount	Undesirable implications of these commands
"I tell you that anyone who divorces his wife, except for marital unfaithfulness, causes her to become an adulteress, and anyone who marries the divorced woman commits adultery" (Matthew 5:32).	To set such stringent standards for divorce and remarriage does not appear to be in the earthly best interests of the men who recorded this saying.
"I tell you, Do not resist an evil person. If someone strikes you on the right cheek, turn to him the other also. And if someone wants to sue you and take your tunic, let him have your cloak as well. If someone forces you to go one mile, go with him two miles. Give to the one who asks you, and do not turn away from the one who wants to borrow from you" (Matthew 5:39–42).	To not resist the insults of an evil person is to resist our basic human instincts; it also sets up an inconvenient standard of behavior for the apostles, who were undergoing persecution when this saying was written down.
"I tell you: Love your enemies and pray for those who persecute you, that you may be sons of your Father in heaven" (Matthew 5:44, 45).	To pray for our enemies goes well beyond any ethic ever uttered and commands kindness where enmity is natural.
"Be perfect … as your heavenly Father is perfect" (Matthew 5:48).	To be perfect is an unattainable request for fallible human beings.

Excerpts from The Sermon on the Mount	Undesirable implications of these commands
"Do not store up for yourselves treasures on earth, where moth and rust destroy, and where thieves break in and steal. But store up for yourselves treasures in heaven, where moth and rust do not destroy, and where thieves do not break in and steal. For where your treasure is, there your heart will be also" (Matthew 6:19–21).	To not accumulate financial wealth contradicts our deepest desires for temporal security.
"Do not judge, or you too will be judged. For in the same way you judge others, you will be judged, and with the measure you use, it will be measured to you" (Matthew 7:1, 2).	To not judge unless our own lives are in order counters our natural tendency to point out faults in others.

Jesus' commands don't qualify for those seeking a user-friendly religion. Geisler states, "These commands clearly are not the commands that people would impose on themselves. Who can live up to such standards? Only a perfect person. Perhaps that's exactly the point."[55] The Bible is demanding and makes it obvious that we could not adhere to such standards. In effect, its abundantly clear message is that such a lifestyle would require an advocate, a helper, even a Savior.

KEY QUOTE

"It ain't those parts of the Bible that I can't understand that bother me, it is the parts that I do understand." — Mark Twain

DYK...

The title Sermon on the Mount doesn't come from the Bible. The Scriptures simply record that Jesus "went up on a mountain, and when He was seated His disciples came to Him" (Matthew 5:1). The "Sermon on the Mount" label was first applied by Augustine, writing a commentary on Matthew in the fourth century. Augustine wrote in Latin, and the phrase did not appear in English until the Coverdale Bible used it in 1535.[56]

LINK TO YOUR LIFE

Caution: in your desire to follow Jesus with all your heart, soul, mind, and strength, you may be tempted to focus on what you are doing rather than on who you are becoming. We are human beings, not human do-ings. And while we are called to act, don't let your service exceed your worship. Listen to Jesus and follow Him wholeheartedly, but do so with a desire to know God, rather than simply complete a checklist.

SMALL GROUP DISCUSSION

Anything particular resonate with you from this chapter? What are the most challenging aspects of the Christian life? Do you think it's important to discuss aspects from this chapter with friends interested in Christianity? Why or why not?

KEY VERSE

"Anyone who wants to be my disciple must follow me, because my servants must be where I am. And the Father will honor anyone who serves me" (John 12:26, NLT).

PRAYER

"God, I want to live a no-excuse life for you. It is a high calling to follow you. Thank you for the invitation. Help me be the person you've called me to be so I can serve you in ways that honor and please you.

Continue your prayer:

Amen."

Sixteen
The Bible Is ... HISTORICAL

OK, I admit it. I'm particularly fond of this chapter because I like charts and, frankly, this chapter has an impressive one. The chart screams loud and clear that the Bible is a historical document, not an example of historical fiction. The New Testament writers include more than 30 historically confirmed people in their writings. And as the chart below reveals, the figures are not just acknowledged by biblical writers. Instead, non-biblical sources authenticate the Bible's historical account.

This is particularly significant when comparing the Bible to other religious books, such as *The Book of Mormon*. In Lee Strobel's *The Case for Christ*, he writes, "Although Joseph Smith, the founder of the Mormon church, claimed that his *Book of Mormon* is 'the most correct of any book upon the earth,' archaeology has repeatedly failed to substantiate its claims about events that supposedly occurred long ago in the Americas."[57] Later, Strobel quotes authors John Ankerberg and John Weldon, who claim, "No *Book of Mormon* cities have ever been located, no *Book of Mormon* person, place, nation, or name has ever been found, no *Book of Mormon* artifacts, no *Book of Mormon* scriptures, no Book of Mormon inscriptions . . . nothing which demonstrates the *Book of*

Mormon is anything other than myth or invention has ever been found."[58]

Contrast that with reliable biblical accounts. The New Testament would've lost credibility with its contemporary audience had it used the names of real people in a fictional account. The writers would've been quickly exposed as frauds for inserting the names of real people in fictitious accounts. Instead, contemporary historians of the New Testament era confirmed its accuracy. The Bible is a reliable, historical document.

New Testament Figures Cited by Non-Christian Writers and/or Confirmed Through Archaeology[59]

Person	NT Citation	Non-Christian Source(s)
Jesus	many citations	Josephus, Tacitus, Pliny the Younger, Phlegon, Thallus, Suetonius, Lucian, Celsus, Mara Bar-Serapion, The Jewish Talmud
Agrippa I	Acts 12:1–24	Philo, Josephus
Agrippa II	Acts 25:13–26:32	coins, Josephus
Ananias	Acts 23:2; 24:1	Josephus
Annas	Luke 3:2; John 18:13, 24; Acts 4:6	Josephus
Aretas	2 Corinthians 11:32	Josephus
Bernice (wife of Agrippa II)	Acts 23:13	Josephus
Caesar Augustus	Luke 2:1	Josephus and others
Caiaphas	several citations	An ossuary, Josephus
Claudius	Acts 11:28; 18:2	Josephus

Person	NT Citation	Non-Christian Source(s)
Drusilla (wife of Felix)	Acts 24:24	Josephus
Egyptian false prophet	Acts 21:38	Josephus
Erastus	Acts 19:22	inscription
Felix	Acts 23:24–25:14	Tacitus, Josephus
Gallio	Acts 18:12–17	inscription
Gamaliel	Acts 5:34; 22:3	Josephus
Herod Antipas	Matthew 14:1–12; Mark 6:14–29; Luke 3:1; 23:7–12	Josephus
Herod Archelaus	Matthew 2:22	Josephus
Herod the Great	Matthew 2:1–19; Luke 1:5	Tacitus, Josephus
Herod Philip I	Matthew 14:3; Mark 6:17	Josephus
Herod Philip II	Luke 3:1	Josephus
Herodias	Matthew 14:3; Mark 6:17	Josephus
Herodias's daughter (Salome)	Matthew 14:1–12; Mark 6:14–29	Josephus
James	several citations	Josephus
John the Baptist	several citations	Josephus
Judas the Galilean	Acts 5:37	Josephus
Lysanias	Luke 3:1	inscription, Josephus
Pilate	several citations	inscription, coins, Josephus, Philo, Tacitus
Quirinius	Luke 2:2	Josephus
Porcius Festus	Acts 24:27–26:32	Josephus
Sergius Paulus	Acts 13:6–12	inscription
Tiberius Caesar	Luke 3:1	Luke 3:1 Tacitus, Suetonius, Paterculus, Dio Cassius, Josephus

KEY QUOTE

"After trying to shatter the historicity and validity of the Scripture, I came to the conclusion that it is historically trustworthy. If one discards the Bible as being unreliable, then one must discard almost all literature of antiquity. One problem I constantly face is the desire on the part of many to apply one standard or test to secular literature and another to the Bible. One must apply the same test, whether the literature under investigation is secular or religious. Having done this, I believe we can hold the Scriptures in our hands and say, "The Bible is trustworthy and historically reliable."[60] — Josh McDowell

DYK . . .

A Roman satirist named Lucian gives a historical reference to Jesus. His sarcasm would easily get him an appearance on David Letterman or Conan or Leno were he alive today.

> "The Christians, you know, worship a man to this day — the distinguished personage who introduced their novel rites, and was crucified on that account. . . . You see, these misguided creatures start with the general conviction that they are immortal for all time, which explains the contempt of death and voluntary self-devotion which are so common among them; and then it was impressed on them by their original lawgiver that they are all brothers, from the moment they are converted, and deny the gods of Greece, and worship the crucified sage, and live after his laws. All this they take quite on faith, with the result that they despise all worldly goods alike, regarding them as common property."[61]

LINK TO YOUR LIFE

The Bible isn't dust-worthy. It's the same book that has transformed human lives for thousands of years. And get this: God wrote it. Be grateful to have such an amazing gift and read it today.

SMALL GROUP DISCUSSION

What value — if any — is there regarding the Bible's historical roots? Does it impact your view of the Bible in any way? How so?

KEY VERSE

"An honest witness tells the truth, but a false witness tells lies" (Proverbs 12:17).

PRAYER

"God, your love is amazing and your grace immeasurable. Because of that, it's no wonder people doubt the words of the Bible. But thank you for its truth.

Continue your prayer:

Amen."

Seventeen
The Bible Is . . . INCLUSIVE

One criticism of God's salvation offer is that it's "exclusive": only people who place their faith in Jesus can have a relationship with God. While God's salvation plan does go through Jesus, He invites everyone to come. Actually, He cares so much that Peter describes it this way: "The Lord is not slow in keeping his promise, as some understand slowness. Instead he is patient with you, not wanting anyone to perish, but everyone to come to repentance" (2 Peter 3:9). God's offer is, in fact, inclusive, and He's doing all He can to let everyone respond.

Similarly, the Bible's message is inclusive. It allows for multiple accounts to describe the same biblical events. This is most often seen when comparing the gospels. While some criticize the gospel writers for having contradictory content, the critics are incorrect. Matthew's gospel (Matthew 20:29-34) mentions the healing of two blind men while Mark (10:46-52) and Luke (18:35-43) describe only one, but this does not prove them to be contradictory. Instead, they are complementary. Matthew mentions two men while Luke and Mark write of the more prominent of the two men. The gospel writers provide independent eyewitness accounts. The key themes or elements are in agreement, but the individual details may differ.

This can be experienced tonight on the evening news, or right now with an internet search of a current event. All news agencies will report on the same hot topic, but the details, perspectives, and views will vary according to the personality of the writer or audience being addressed.

The four gospel accounts offer complementary views, providing greater understanding of a single event. And in doing so, the reliability of the Bible is strengthened, as we can have confidence the writers did not meet together to confirm a uniform story. Geisler and Turek concur: "In light of the numerous divergent details in the New Testament, it's clear that the New Testament writers didn't get together to smooth out their testimonies. This means they certainly were not trying to pass off a lie as the truth. For if they were making up the New Testament story, they would have gotten together to make sure they were consistent in every detail. Such harmonization clearly didn't happen, and this confirms the genuine eyewitness nature of the New Testament and the independence of each writer."[62]

The Bible's inclusive content allows for many views of the same inclusive message: all are welcome.

KEY QUOTE

"The bottom line is this: agreement on the major points and divergence on the minor details is the nature of eyewitness testimony, and this is the very nature of the New Testament documents."[63] — Norm Geisler and Frank Turek

DYK...

Simon Greenleaf, the Harvard law professor who wrote the standard study on what constitutes legal evidence, credited his own conversion to Christianity as having come from his careful examination of the Gospel witnesses. If anyone knew the characteristics of genuine eyewitness testimony, it was Greenleaf. He concluded that the four Gospels "would have been received in evidence in any court of justice, without the slightest hesitation."[64]

LINK TO YOUR LIFE

You will hear people insist that the Bible is unreliable because it is filled with contradictions. Always ask for specific examples, including book, chapter, and verse. It's easy to claim something is untrue, but it's another to provide valid support. If someone provides an example or two that stump you, don't worry! It just means you've got some homework to do. There are numerous resources that address specific common "contradictions." These will be valuable tools for your library:

When Critics Ask: A Popular Handbook on Bible Difficulties, Norm Geisler and Thomas Howe

Hard Sayings of the Bible, Walter Keiser Jr. and F.F. Bruce

Answers to Tough Questions: A Survey of Problem Passages and Issues, J. Carl Laney

Now, That's a Good Question, R.C. Sproul

Always see a "problem passage" as an opportunity to learn. Quite often, the issues can be resolved with a better understanding of the Bible's culture, geography, or language.

SMALL GROUP DISCUSSION

Where do you stand on this position? Is the Bible inclusive or exclusive? Explain why it is or isn't possible to be both.

KEY VERSE

"Above all, you must realize that no prophecy in Scripture ever came from the prophet's own understanding, or from human initiative. No, those prophets were moved by the Holy Spirit, and

they spoke from God" (2 Peter 1:20, 21, NLT).

PRAYER

"God, thank you for all the people you used to write the Bible. Help me gain a better understanding of you each time I read your word.

Continue your prayer:

Amen."

Eighteen
The Bible Is . . . SCRUTINIZED

Ever wonder if the email offer you received is real or a scam? Is it possible to get a free gift card from Dunkin Donuts . . . or Target . . . or Sam's Club . . . or Costco . . . just for clicking a link? How about the 100 Facebook shares so a child can receive a free heart transplant? Did the infant born in-flight really get free air travel for the rest of his life? Inquiring minds want to know! Fortunately, a Google search on your topic usually offers a reality check, as does a visit to an investigative website like urbanlegends.about.com. The key is to check the facts. Or in the words of the great Sherlock Homes, "I never guess. It is a shocking habit — destructive to the logical faculty."

Ever wonder if the Bible stories are true? The Bible's writers were dealing with the miraculous, so they expected resistance. And they challenged their readers to check the facts.

- Luke introduces his gospel by insuring the Roman official Theophilus that he has provided a careful investigation of the facts in his "orderly account" so that Theophilus could be certain of the things Luke wrote (Luke 1:1-4).
- Peter claims that he didn't believe some cleverly devised story, but he himself was an eyewitness (2 Peter 1:16) of the things

he wrote.

- In Acts 26, Paul was called insane by Festus, Governor of Judea. Paul counters by saying "the king is familiar with these things" and "none of this has escaped his notice, because it was not done in a corner." In other words, Festus — or anyone — can check the facts.
- In 1 Corinthians 15, Paul reminds the church that after Jesus' resurrection he appeared to several people, including "more than five hundred of the brothers and sisters at the same time, most of whom are still living." Paul was saying to his readers: If you don't believe me, do your homework and check the facts, particularly since most are still living.
- In 2 Corinthians 12, Paul claims to have done miracles when he was with them previously. He'd be a fool to suggest such a thing if it were not true.

The Bible's writers could have had a pompous attitude, demanding to be taken seriously since they were speaking on behalf of God. But God knew that attitude would have limited staying power, particularly in our current skeptical age. So, time and time again, the Bible's authors reminded readers that they or those they were connected to were eyewitnesses and, therefore, accountable. If there were any doubts or questions about what they professed, there were enough living witnesses who could deny their report if necessary.

The Bible is scrutinized, or, at the very least, provides plenty of opportunity for thorough investigation. When you check the facts, you discover the Bible is reliable.

KEY QUOTE

"Some of the New Testament writers were not apostles. How can we explain their authority? They used the apostolic message which was 'confirmed to us by those who heard' (Hebrews 2:3). Mark worked closely with Peter (1 Peter 5:13); James and Jude were

closely associated with the apostles in Jerusalem and were probably Jesus' brothers; Luke was a companion of Paul (2 Timothy 4:11) who interviewed many eyewitnesses to produce his account (Luke 1:1-4). Paul's writings are even equated with Scripture by Peter (2 Peter 3:15, 16). In each case (with the exception of Hebrews; we don't know for sure who wrote that book), there is a definite link between the writer and the apostles who gave them information."[65]
– Norman Geisler

DYK . . .

James MacDonald writes, "It goes without saying that the Bible is ever and always under attack. Since the Old and New Testaments were written, people have given their lives to destroy God's Word. The irrefutable record of the Bible's survival despite this onslaught is evidence that it is a supernatural book. No other book has been so burned and banned and outlawed as the Bible. From Roman emperors to Communist leaders to college professors, many have taken it upon themselves to attack God's book. Why this book? Why are people always attacking the Bible? Travel to any state school in America and try to find someone attacking the *Koran*. No, instead they talk about that book with respect. Check out a secular college campus and try to find someone attacking the *Book of Mormon*. Why is no one doing that? Because almighty God has only written one book that convicts people of their sin and the necessity of being reconciled to Him."[66]

LINK TO YOUR LIFE

Unfortunately, because of the age in which we live, we cannot interview eyewitnesses to biblical events. Fortunately, as revealed throughout previous chapters, history speaks, as archaeological evidence abounds for the reliability of the Bible. At some point, however, it becomes a faith decision. It is faith built on a solid foundation of fact, but faith nonetheless. Will you believe the Bible is the word of God? In Billy Graham's autobiography, he tells the story of his crisis of faith while walking on a beach. He had to draw a literal line in the sand and decide whether or not he believed the Bible to be from God. Thankfully, he did, and millions have been positively impacted by his ministry.

There is a new line before you. Will you cross it, believing our scrutinized Bible to be true?

SMALL GROUP DISCUSSION

In what ways have you ever doubted the Bible to be true? Are there particular stories you've questioned? How has this chapter encouraged you or at least piqued your interest?

KEY VERSE

Jesus replied, "Your mistake is that you don't know the Scriptures, and you don't know the power of God" (Matthew 22:29, NLT).

PRAYER

"God, today I affirm the Bible is your word and therefore my guide for life. Thank you for speaking to me. Help me obey your word.

Continue your prayer:

Amen."

Nineteen

The Bible Is . . . SIMPLE and CLEAR

"But wait! There's more! If you order *RIGHT NOW*, we'll give you twice as much. That's double the value!!"

Technology is wonderful, but it means we have to endure the dreaded infomercial. From Bowflex to ShamWow to the Snuggie, television crews and boisterous pitchmen and women have invaded our homes. They've learned the art of crafting a story so enticing it motivates us to pick up the phone . . . since operators are standing by! Of course, the reality of the infomercial is just one reason for our biblical skepticism. The Bible's message is too good to be true, we assume, so it has to be made up. It's a message of hope built on hype. The gospel writers probably had a field day describing the resurrection. Or did they?

The Gospel of Peter is not a biblical book. It was written more than 100 years after the resurrection of Jesus and includes a description of the resurrection featuring a walking and talking cross and the heads of men stretching all the way to heaven. It makes for good reading, but not accurate history. On the contrary, the four gospel accounts of the resurrection offer nothing extravagant in their description. Granted, the bodily resurrection of Jesus Christ is impressive — miraculous even — but that's not the point. The way in which it is described is low profile compared with how products are marketed today. The language is matter-of-fact — even *bland* — nothing dramatic or bizarre. This is significant because the resurrection is the gospel writer's signature event. If ever there were a time to spice things up a bit, to prove a point, this would be it. Norm Geisler believes the writers' theological constraint is evidence of their desire to get history correct. They knew the facts would speak for themselves. There was no reason to tell anything but the truth. The message of the Bible is consistently simple and clear.

And by the way, the makers of the Ab Rocket want you to know that with just five minutes a day with their product, your abs will be transformed from flab to fab.

I'm thinking the Bible has a more convincing and winning argument than that.

KEY QUOTE

"If you go to most evangelical church services today, the constant emphasis is 'come to Jesus to get saved.' That is certainly taught in the whole of the New Testament, but it's hardly mentioned in the Gospels. Why? Because the Gospel writers were writing history, not mere theology. Of course New Testament history has dramatic implications on theology, but those implications are drawn out in other New Testament writings, namely the Epistles (letters). It would have been easy for the Gospel writers to interject the theological implications of every historical event, but they didn't. They were eyewitnesses who were writing history, not fiction writers or proselytizing theologians."[67] — Norm Geisler and Frank Turek

DYK...

"Their levelheadedness [the gospel writers] is also on display with the other miracles they record," write Geisler and Turek. "The thirty-five other miracles attributed to Jesus in the Gospels are described as if from reporters, not wild-eyed preachers. The Gospel writers don't offer flamboyant descriptions or fire and brimstone commentary — just the facts."[68]

LINK TO YOUR LIFE

There are no hidden messages or secret treasure maps tucked away in your Bible. It's the Word of God in plain language. On one level that's not exciting, because it would be great to discover something never before seen. But don't miss the big picture: it's the Word of God! You don't have to wonder if you're "getting it right." Instead you can be confident there is no great mystery. The truth is God has spoken and wants you to respond. Open your Bible with great expectation. The God of the universe wants to talk to you.

SMALL GROUP DISCUSSION

What would you say is the simple, clear message of the Bible? Do churches cloud things up from time to time? What advice would you give to pastors to help prevent that?

KEY VERSE

"And if Christ has not been raised, your faith is futile; you are still in your sins" (1 Corinthians 15:17).

PRAYER

"God, I sometimes forget that the Bible is your message to me. I often see the Bible as just words on a page. Give me daily reminders that you have something to teach me. I want to open my Bible with enthusiasm.

Continue your prayer:

Amen."

Twenty
The Bible Is . . . LIFE-CHANGING

The Bible's truths are life-changing. So much so that radical shifts were made in Jewish beliefs. In Lee Strobel's *The Case for Christ*, Dr. J.P. Moreland discussed the longstanding traditions of Jewish culture that had been passed down for generations during the time of Christ. Despite being persecuted by the Babylonians, Assyrians, Persians, Greeks, and Romans, Jewish culture prevailed "because the things that made the Jews, Jews were unbelievably important to them. They believed these institutions were entrusted to them by God. They believed that to abandon these institutions would be to risk their souls being damned to hell after death."[69]

Yet Jesus arrives on the scene, invites people to follow him, and weeks after He's crucified, thousands of Jews are following him, proclaiming Him to be Savior, and adhering to a new set of beliefs — monumental shifts in beliefs.

Pre-Resurrection Belief[70]	Post-Resurrection Belief
Animal sacrifice	Unnecessary because of Christ's sacrifice
Binding Law of Moses	Nonbinding because it was fulfilled by Christ's life

Pre-Resurrection Belief[70]	Post-Resurrection Belief
Strict monotheism	Trinity (three persons in one divine presence)
The Sabbath	Replaced by Sunday (first day of week) worship
Conquering Messiah	Sacrificial Messiah (he'll conquer when he returns)
Circumcision	Replaced by baptism and Communion

Besides Jewish adherence to a new set of beliefs, more life change is evidenced by the apostles and writers of the New Testament. They were persecuted and martyred when they could have easily saved themselves by rejecting Jesus. They chose to be crucified, stoned, beheaded, or exiled instead. Chuck Colson, aide to President Nixon, went to prison for his involvement in the Watergate scandal. He compared his and his colleagues' Watergate experience with those of the apostles:

"I have been challenged myself many times on the resurrection. My answer is always that the disciples and five hundred others gave eyewitness accounts of seeing Jesus, risen from the tomb. But then I'm asked, 'How do you know they were telling the truth? Maybe they were perpetrating a hoax.' My answer to that comes from an unlikely source: Watergate.

Watergate involved a conspiracy to cover up a crime, perpetuated by the closest aides to the President of the United States — the most powerful men in America — who were intensely loyal to their president. But one of them, John Dean, turned state's evidence, that is, testified against Nixon, as he put it, 'to save his own skin' — and he did so only two weeks after informing the president about what was really going on — two weeks! The real cover-up, the lie, could only be held together for two weeks, and then everybody else jumped ship in order to save themselves. Now, the fact is that all those around the president were facing was embarrassment, maybe prison. Nobody's life was at stake. But what about the disciples? Twelve powerless men, peasants really, were facing not just embarrassment or political disgrace, but beatings, stoning, execution. Every single one of the disciples insisted, to their dying breaths, that they had physically seen Jesus bodily raised from the dead.

Don't you think that one of those apostles would have cracked before being beheaded or stoned? That one of them would have made a deal with the authorities? None did. You see, men will give their lives for something they believe to be true — they will never give their lives for something they know to be false."[71]

News stories abound with proof that people will die for a lie they believe to be true. But it is not possible that a person, or group, or thousands of people would live lives of ridicule and abuse — under the threat of death — for what they know is a lie. Jesus has risen. He has risen indeed. And the message of the Bible continues to offer life change.

KEY QUOTE

"Supreme Court Justice Antonin Scalia pointed out the absurdity of those who doubt the historicity of the New Testament. In a remark biting with sarcasm against modern-day intellectuals, Scalia stated exactly what we've been saying regarding the motives of the New Testament writers. Namely, since the New Testament writers had nothing to gain and everything to lose, we ought to believe what they say about the Resurrection. Scalia declared, 'It is not irrational to accept the testimony of eyewitnesses who had nothing to gain. . . . The [worldly] wise do not believe in the resurrection of the dead. So everything from Easter morning to the Ascension had to be made up by the groveling enthusiasts as part of their plan to get themselves martyred."[72] — Norman Geisler

DYK . . .

Muslims have been willing to die for what they believe. Yet, as professor and philosopher Dr. J.P. Moreland notes, they choose to die "for their belief that Allah revealed himself to Muhammad, but this revelation was not done in a publicly observable way. So they could be wrong about it. However, the apostles were willing to die for something they had seen with their own eyes and touched with their own hands. And when you've got eleven credible people with no ulterior motives, with nothing to gain and a lot to lose, who all agree they observed something with their own eyes — now you've got some difficulty explaining that away."[73]

LINK TO YOUR LIFE

Life change is optional . . . it's your option. Sure, the Bible can be confusing from time to time, but more often than not it is clear. But what isn't as clear is your commitment. Choose today to follow God and look to His Bible for direction.

SMALL GROUP DISCUSSION

What life change have you seen in your life? Share what life change you've seen in the lives of others in your group, or mutual friends you might know. Share a way for people to pray for more change in your life.

KEY VERSE

"But if you refuse to serve the Lord, then choose today whom you will serve. Would you prefer the gods your ancestors served beyond the Euphrates? Or will it be the gods of the Amorites in whose land you now live? But as for me and my family, we will serve the Lord" (Joshua 24:15, NLT).

PRAYER

"God, I want life change. I don't only want what I've experienced in the past. I want life change today and tomorrow. May your Holy Spirit empower me to follow you.

Continue your prayer:

Amen."

SECTION 2: God is . . .

Twenty-one
God Is . . . MORE Than You Can IMAGINE

Names matter. Whether you're Juliet questioning the consequence of Romeo's last name or a world-class communicator claiming a person's name is the "sweetest and most important sound in any language," names matter. And the name of God is no different.

In fact, there are many names of God found in the Bible. While that may appear confusing, it actually makes sense because God cannot be confined or described with one word. God is more than you can imagine. A few of His names are listed below, but the one name God uses to identify *Himself* comes from the book of Exodus. In chapter 3, Moses is intimidated by the task God has set before him. When Moses asks under what authority he should say he's under, God replies, "I am who I am. This is what you are to say to the Israelites: 'I am has sent me to you'" (Exodus 3:14). Huh? I am? While it may sound a little too close to Popeye's "I yam what I yam," it's no joke, and we can be thankful. I Am, translated Yahweh in Hebrew, is profound and life-giving. Consider what the following scholars say:

- The meaning is that God is the self-existent One. As Ronald Allen states, "He exists dependent upon nothing or no one excepting his own will."[74]

- The words "I am" refer not to God's static being but to His active existence. He is actively involved with humanity, responding to their needs and revealing His person. He exists not only for His own sake, but also for the sake of His people.[75]
- Walther Eichrodt commented that the words "I am" mean that God is "really and truly present, ready to help and to act."[76]

Wow! That sounds amazing. I love the connection of God's name both to His being and to His availability. The context of Moses' intimidation and fear is the perfect unveiling of not only who God is but what God provides. I need a "right now" God who is ready to act.

But wait, there's more! Take a look at this short list (really, there are many more) of names for God found in the Bible.

El Shaddai	Almighty One	Genesis 17:1
El Elyon	Most High God	Genesis 14:9
El Olam	Everlasting God	Genesis 21:33
El Roi	The God who sees	Genesis 16:13
Yahweh Jireh	the Lord will provide	Genesis 22:14
Yahweh Nissi	the Lord is my banner	Exodus 17:15
Yahweh Shalom	the Lord is peace	Judges 6:24
Yahweh Maccaddeshcem	the Lord who sanctifies you	Exodus 31:13
Yahweh Roi	the Lord is my shepherd	Psalm 23:1
Yahweh Elohim Israel	the Lord, the God of Israel	Judges 5:3

Strictly speaking, the compounds above are not additional names of God, but designations or titles that often grew out of commemorative events. However, they do reveal additional facets of the character of God.[77]

KEY QUOTE

"We desire to know God — yes; but not merely that we may have knowledge, it is also that we may come into conformity with Him and with His plan for our lives. We also remind ourselves that in order to know God, we are entirely dependent upon God's revelation of Himself." [78] — D.M. Lloyd-Jones

DYK . . .

"Since *Yahweh* was God's personal name by which He was known to Israel, in post-exilic times it began to be considered so sacred that it was not pronounced. Instead the term *Adonai* was usually substituted, and by the sixth to seventh centuries AD the vowels of *Adonai* were combined with the consonants *YHWH* to remind the synagogue reader to pronounce the sacred name as *Adonai*. From this came the artificial word *Jehovah*."[79]

And, if you have Jewish friends, you may note that they never spell the word 'God.' Instead, out of respect, they'll write G_d.

LINK TO YOUR LIFE

Our minds are powerful. Got questions whether or not God can or will come through? We need to make sure we're thinking correctly about who God is. Usually, our view of god is small (lowercase 'g'), but that's faulty thinking. When facing a challenge, or simply preparing for a new day, it's critical we know God (capital 'G'). And until God's promises fail, take God at his word that he will follow through on his promises.

SMALL GROUP DISCUSSION

How have you seen the MORE side of God in your life? In what ways do you want or need God to provide more? Take time to thank God as a group.

KEY VERSE

"I am the Lord; that is my name! I will not yield my glory to another or my praise to idols" (Isaiah 42:8).

PRAYER

"God, you are, and you will always be. Give me reminders today that no matter where I go, there you will be.

Continue your prayer:

Amen."

Twenty-two
God Is . . . TRIUNE

Let's start with the obvious: the Trinity is complex. While it makes sense conceptually, it's confusing logically. John Wesley said it best: "Bring me a worm that can comprehend a man, and then I will show you a man that can comprehend the triune God!" Similarly, St. Augustine, while puzzling over the doctrine of the Trinity, was walking along the beach one day when he observed a young boy with a bucket, running back and forth to pour water into a little hole. Augustine asked, "What are you doing?" The boy replied, "I'm trying to put the ocean into this hole." Then Augustine realized that he had been trying to put an infinite God into his finite mind.[80]

There are scholars with more degrees than Fahrenheit who struggle to understand and communicate this important teaching. To make things more confusing, the word Trinity is not found in the Bible. The concept, however, is exceedingly prevalent. The Bible teaches that there is one God who has revealed Himself in three persons, God the Father, God the Son, and God the Holy Spirit. Each functions as God, in distinct yet harmonious ways. We will look at the deity of Jesus and the Holy Spirit in subsequent chapters. Yet the Trinity presents two key concepts: "threeness" and oneness.

A key Old Testament passage and Judaism's basic confession of faith is the Shema, Deuteronomy 6:4, which emphasizes the unity of God: "Hear, O Israel: The Lord our God, the Lord is one." Probably the verse that best states the doctrine of the triunity of God balancing both aspects of the concept, the unity and the Trinity, is Matthew 28:19: "baptizing them in the name of the Father, and of the Son, and of the Holy Spirit." There is no question about the "threeness" aspect, for the Father, Son, and Spirit are mentioned — and only three. The unity is strongly indicated in the singular "name" rather than "names."[81]

There is no perfect illustration of the Trinity, but there have been many attempts. A classic diagram reveals the following:

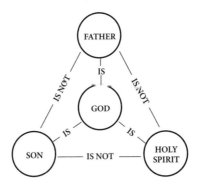

Bruce Bicekl and Stan Jantz provide three illustrations from nature:

1) The Apple — Although an apple is one in essence, it has three distinct parts: the skin, the meat, and the seeds. Each part is unique, yet we know the apple is a complete entity.

2) The Egg — An egg also has three parts: the shell, the white, and the yolk. Again, each part serves a different function, but each part is all egg, and the egg is one in essence.

3) Water — Water commonly exists in three forms: ice (solid) is water; water (liquid) is water; and steam (gas) is water. But whatever the form, it's the same H2O molecule.[82]

Even Mark Twain put creative energy in communicating the concept in his work *Three Thousand Years Among the Microbes*: "Water is an individual, an animal, and is alive, remove the hydrogen and it is an animal and is alive; the remaining oxygen is also an individual, an animal, and is alive. Recapitulation: the two individuals combined constitute a third individual — and yet each continues to be an individual . . . here was mute Nature explaining the sublime mystery of the Trinity so luminously that even the commonest understanding could comprehend it, whereas many a trained master of words had labored to do it with speech and failed."

The concept of a Triune God is complex, yet important, because it provides a greater understanding to how our salvation is accomplished, and it gives us a greater view of God. Although God has made Himself known to us, God remains yet unfathomable.

KEY QUOTE

"Tell me how it is that in this room there are three candles and but one light, and I will explain to you the mode of the divine existence."[83] — John Wesley

DYK . . .

When you attend a wedding you are witnessing a miracle. Not only are you witnessing a covenant when vows are exchanged, but you are watching the binding of the husband and wife together for life. The miracle of oneness takes place before your eyes as two people actually become one. Genesis 2:24 says, "For this reason a man will leave his father and mother and be united to his wife, and they will become one flesh." Although the husband and wife "retain their own individuality and personhood, in a mystical but real way they would be indissolubly united into one spiritual entity."[84]

LINK TO YOUR LIFE

There are some celebrities and professionals who are so busy they have multiple assistants. Well, with the triunity of God, you have God's assistance in your life exhibited in multiple ways. God the Father created the plan of salvation, God the Son fulfilled the Father's plan, and God the Spirit applies the plan to your life. All three persons of the triune God are committed to helping you be the person God created you to be. So the good news is that if you've got an issue, got a question, or got a problem, you can call on God. But the better news is that even if you don't think you have questions or problems, God is still at work in your life in a variety of ways.

SMALL GROUP DISCUSSION

Has the concept of the Trinity done anything for your faith? Does it encourage you or confuse you . . . or do you just not think about it? Should it be important? Why?

KEY VERSE

"May the grace of the Lord Jesus Christ, and the love of God, and the fellowship of the Holy Spirit be with you all" (2 Corinthians 13:14).

PRAYER

"God, you are awesome. Thank you for your immense involvement in my life. Help me get a greater understanding of how mighty and majestic you are.

Continue your prayer:

Amen."

Twenty-three
God Is . . . NEAR

God created us and hasn't left us. Psalm 139:13 says, "You made all the delicate, inner parts of my body and knit me together in my mother's womb (NLT)." Our traits and personality reflect God's handiwork. His never-ending presence reveals His character. "The technical term used to speak of God's involvement in creation is the word *immanent,* meaning 'remaining in' creation. The God of the Bible is no abstract deity removed from, and uninterested in his creation. The Bible is the story of God's involvement with his creation, and particularly the people in it."[85]

But you and I are only as close to God as we want to be. A farmer's wife leaned against the passenger door in her husband's beloved pickup truck as they drove into town. She asked, "How come we never sit side by side in this old truck of yours anymore? I remember driving into town as newlyweds, practically glued to your side." Without taking his eyes off the road, the farmer replied in two words, "You moved." James 4:8 illustrates God's desire: "Come near to God, and he will come near to you."

Whether we decide to stay connected to God or not, He chooses to stay near. For some, that brings peace. For others, anxiety. But when factoring in God's commitment regardless of our condition, it's the ultimate sign of love. Gary Inrig illustrates the magnitude of God's acceptance when writing about the soldier who phoned his parents that he was on his way home. His parents hadn't heard from him in months and were ecstatic.

"Mom, I just wanted to let you know that I'm bringing a buddy home with me. He got hurt pretty bad, and he only has one eye, one arm, and one leg. I'd sure like him to live with us."

"Sure son," his mother replied. "He sounds like a brave man. We can find room for him for a while."

"Mom, you don't understand. I want him to come live with us."

"Well, OK," she finally said. "We could try it for six months or so."

"No, Mom, I want him to stay always. He needs us. He's only got one eye, one arm, and one leg. He's really in bad shape."

By now his mother had lost her patience. "Son, you're being unrealistic about this. You're emotional because you've been in a war. That boy will be a drag on you and a constant problem for all of us. Be reasonable."

The phone clicked dead. The next day, the parents got a notification: their son had committed suicide. A week later the parents received the body. They looked down with unspeakable sorrow on the corpse of their son — who had one eye, one arm, and one leg."[86]

God is aware of all that is going on in our lives, for better or worse. And regardless of our condition, King David writes that "The Lord is close to the brokenhearted and saves those who are crushed in spirit" (Psalm 34:18). No matter who you are, what you've done or how you feel, take courage: God is near.

KEY QUOTE

"It is important to distinguish the biblical doctrine of God's omnipresence from the false view of pantheism. Omnipresence states that God is present everywhere, though separate from the world and the things in it. Pantheism, on the other hand, teaches that God is in everything. The Bible affirms that God is present with you as you read this book, whereas pantheism teaches that God is in the chair in which you're sitting. Pantheism distorts the doctrine of God's immanence (presence) by failing to recognize that God is active in His creation, but is not to be identified with it."[87] — J. Carl Laney

DYK . . .

"The doctrine of divine immanence has ecological application. We should have an appreciation for all that God has created. Nature is not something that is there as a brute fact, something that may be plundered for our purposes. It also has implications regarding our attitudes to fellow humans. God is genuinely present within everyone (although not in the special sense in which he indwells Christians). Therefore, people are not to be despised or treated disrespectfully. A way to show our love for God is to treat lovingly the various members of the creation within which he dwells and works."[88]

LINK TO YOUR LIFE

Take a few days and write out your prayers to God. Pray as you write, offering all that is on your mind and heart to God. Of course God already knows what is going on in your life — He is near — but He wants you to stay connected and close. Tell God everything that's going on. He wants to help. Writing out your prayer provides a record so that you can go back and review how God answers.

SMALL GROUP DISCUSSION

Share with the group a time you felt God was near. How does a memory like that impact your faith? Do you think God is near more than you're aware? Explain.

KEY VERSE

"Where can I go from your Spirit?
Where can I flee from your presence?
If I go up to the heavens, you are there;
if I make my bed in the depths, you are there.
If I rise on the wings of the dawn,
if I settle on the far side of the sea,
even there your hand will guide me,
your right hand will hold me fast" (Psalm 139:7-10).

PRAYER

"God, thank you that you are here, that you are near, and because of that, I don't have to fear.

Continue your prayer:

Amen."

Twenty-four
God Is . . . FAR

Saying God is far makes Him out to be impersonal and aloof. Nothing could be further from the truth. The theological term is *transcendent*, and by this we mean God is separate from His creation and far above it, in the sense that He is superior to it. It also emphasizes that God is distinct from His creation, and not part of it. While we are made in God's image, our similarity stops there. We are God's creation, not His colleague.

Theologian Millard Erickson writes, "Although there are love and trust and openness between us and God, we are not equals. He is the almighty sovereign Lord. We are his servants and followers. This means that we will submit our wills to God; we will not try to make his will conform to ours. Our prayers will also be influenced accordingly. Rather than making demands in our prayers, we will pray as Jesus did: 'Not my will, but thine, be done.'"[89]

The biblical teaching that God is far can easily get pushed aside as an academic distinction. The next time you wonder if God cares about His creation or whether it even matters, reflect on the words from Max Lucado's book, *God Came Near*. In it he reminds us that our all-powerful God is still personal . . . and caring . . . and beautiful.

We wonder, with so many miraculous testimonies around us, how we could escape God. But somehow we do. We live in an art gallery of divine creativity and yet are content to gaze only at the carpet.

Or what is pathetically worse, we demand more. More signs. More proof. More hat tricks. As if God were some vaudeville magician we could summon for a dollar.

How have we grown so deaf? How have we grown so immune to awesomeness? Why are we so reluctant to be staggered or thunderstruck?

Perhaps the frequency of the miracles blinds us to their beauty. After all, what spice is there in a springtime or a tree blossom? Don't the seasons come every year? Aren't there countless seashells just like this one?

Bored, we say Ho-hum and replace the remarkable with the regular, the unbelievable with the anticipated. Science and statistics wave their unmagic wand across the face of life, squelching the oohs and aahs and replacing them with formulas and figures. Would you like to see Jesus? Do you dare be an eyewitness of His Majesty? Then rediscover amazement.

The next time you hear a baby laugh or see an ocean wave, take note. Pause and listen as His Majesty whispers ever so gently, "I'm here."[90]

God is near, yet God is far. For those desiring a logical, God-in-the-box formula, this doesn't make sense. The prophet Isaiah anticipated the challenge:

For this is what the high and exalted One says —
he who lives forever, whose name is holy:
"I live in a high and holy place,

but also with the one who is contrite and lowly in spirit,
to revive the spirit of the lowly
and to revive the heart of the contrite" (Isaiah 57:15).

It's a promise of God's power and closeness, whichever we need,
whenever we need.

KEY QUOTE

"Awareness of God begins with wonder and ends with wonder.
Science without wonder is mere arrogance in disguise. The quest
for knowledge should heighten awareness, not diminish it. It
presses toward light, not the obscurity of the cave. As long as man's
pursuit of knowledge resists the transcendence, it is a charade, a
masquerade. It is not a quest for light but a flight from the light. It
rests in the security of the cave."[91] — R.C. Sproul

DYK . . .

"The Bible teaches both God's immanence [near] and His
transcendence [far]. God is highly exalted over His creation
(Exodus 15:1; Psalm 99:2), but He graciously comes down to assist
and deliver the needy and afflicted (Exodus 3:8; Philippians 2:5–
8)."[92]

LINK TO YOUR LIFE

Take a walk or a drive in silence. If possible, go to a place that
inspires you — the woods . . . the water . . . a museum . . . the top of
a high-rise . . . and be silent. Scan the horizon or woods or works of
art and listen for God. You may not hear a thing, but you might. Be
still before the grandeur of God. Ask God to reveal Himself to you.

SMALL GROUP DISCUSSION

The idea of God being far can be good news and bad. How is
that true? What is your current view of God? How has it changed
in the last year? Five years?

KEY VERSE

"Am I a God who is only close at hand?" says the Lord. "No, I am far away at the same time.

Can anyone hide from me in a secret place? Am I not everywhere in all the heavens and earth?" says the Lord (Jeremiah 23:23, 24, NLT).

PRAYER

"God, the more I learn about you, the more I am humbled. Continue to expand my understanding of who you are. May the knowledge lead me to praise and worship.

Continue your prayer:

Amen."

Twenty-five
God Is . . . GOOD

If God had a yearbook picture, it would be highlighted with this text, I believe, from Psalm 103:
"The Lord is compassionate and gracious,
slow to anger, abounding in love. . . .
He does not treat us as our sins deserve
or repay us according to our iniquities" (Psalm 103:8,10).

The Hebrew word for *good* describes what is pleasant, agreeable, and beneficial. Besides describing God's character, it also describes His actions.[93] God is good, and we are the beneficiaries. This is particularly realized when considering how God interacts with our sin.

God could treat us with justice, giving us exactly what we deserve, but that would leave us hopeless and forever separated from him. God might offer mercy, giving us a little less than we deserve. But when factoring in the weight of sin, that would only provide a temporary reprieve. We'd still be unable to deal with the eternal consequences of our sin. Instead, God extends grace, offering something we *don't deserve*: complete forgiveness. Bill Hybels defines grace as "an outrageous blessing bestowed freely on a totally undeserving recipient."[94] We are those recipients, and when we accept God's offer of forgiveness, our record of sin is erased and our account reads:

PAID IN FULL.

This happens only because God is good.

God is gracious and merciful, but God's goodness means He also acts with:

- Integrity
- Genuineness
- Veracity
- Faithfulness
- Love
- Benevolence
- Persistence

The prophet Nahum offers the sum total of God's goodness:
The Lord is good, a refuge in times of trouble.
He cares for those who trust in him (Nahum 1.7).

The character of God never changes. He is either good, or he isn't. This is an important realization because God's goodness transcends our experience.

When things don't go our way, God is still good. Trust in God today.

KEY QUOTE

"The goodness of God means that God is the final standard of good, and that all that God is and does is worthy of approval."[95] — Wayne Grudem

DYK...

It's easier to embrace God's goodness when we consider the alternative. In John 10:10, Jesus reminds us that while Satan's goal is to steal, kill, and destroy, His purpose is to give us life. Quite a distinction. Jesus then illustrates His goodness by identifying Himself as the Good Shepherd. One commentary writer offers four characteristics that set this Good Shepherd apart from the false or evil shepherds:

- He approaches directly — he enters at the gate.
- He has God's authority — the gatekeeper allows him to enter.
- He meets real needs — the sheep recognize his voice and follow him.
- He has sacrificial love — he is willing to lay down his life for the sheep.[96]

LINK TO YOUR LIFE

When Israel realized all God had provided, the end of Nehemiah 9:25 says they "reveled in God's goodness." They didn't just appreciate or say thank you, they partied loud and long. When was the last time you reveled in the goodness of God? If Israel reveled, so should we! It's time to celebrate and have a party. Live it up, remembering all that God has done.

SMALL GROUP DISCUSSION

Can you think of a time in your life when God was good, even though it may not have appeared that way? What did that do for your faith? How is God good today?

KEY VERSE

"You are good, and what you do is good; teach me your decrees" (Psalm 119:68).

PRAYER

"God, I want to believe you are good, but sometimes I doubt. Help me to remember all the ways you have shown your goodness. Help me trust your word and see evidence from my life.

Continue your prayer:

Amen."

Twenty-six
God Is ... POWERFUL

The Old Testament describes a childless couple named Abraham and Sarah. After years of doing everything they could to have a child, they resigned that no baby would be birthed from Sarah's womb. Then God asked them a question that ought to haunt us:

"Is anything too hard for the Lord?" (Genesis 18:14)

The question arose because Sarah laughed when God promised she would deliver a child. "While a nice gesture from God," Sarah surmised, "clearly He was not aware of my circumstances, nor had he heard my daily prayers uttered for years to have a child." And so she laughed at God's promise. I can relate to Sarah's laugh, especially when it appears that God is inactive. But God's question lingers in my mind: is anything too hard for the Lord?

There's a fancy theological word that describes God's power: omnipotence. It's made up of two words: omni, meaning "all"; and potent, meaning "able to do" and "to have power." So omnipotence means God has all power. If that's the case, it raises a lot of questions. Why is there suffering, and why is there pain, and why does God appear to be silent when I need Him most? It would be unwise to attempt a reply in such a limited space, so I will let God speak for Himself. When Job continued to ask God why he suffered without any relief or response from God, God replied by saying, "Brace yourself like a man; I will question you, and you shall answer me" (Job 40:7). God then rattled off His own set of questions, revealing His powerful and personal nature. Job was humbled by the questions and ultimately got to the place where I want to be: embracing complete faith in God.

Nothing is too hard for God. He has all the power to take care of whatever we need, yet His power is used or withheld in ways that allow us to grow and develop. I may not always initially agree with how God responds, but I'm learning to trust Him more and more. God has everything you need, and God is growing you to become the person He wants you to be.

Norman Geisler and Ron Brooks summarize it well:

> "The argument from Creation proves not only that God exists, but that He has power. Only a God with incredible power could create and sustain the whole universe. His energy would have to be greater than all the energy that was ever available in the whole Creation, for He not only caused all things, He holds them together and keeps them in existence and still sustains His own existence. That is more power than we can imagine."[97]

And it's all the power we'll ever need.

KEY QUOTE

"Look to the canyons to see the Creator's splendor. Touch the flowers and see his delicacy. Listen to the thunder and hear his power. But gaze on [humanity] — the zenith — and witness all three . . . and more."[98] — Max Lucado

DYK . . .

"Ponder the achievement of God.

He doesn't condone our sin, nor does he compromise his standard.

He doesn't ignore our rebellion, nor does he relax his demands.

Rather than dismiss our sin, he assumes our sin and, incredibly, sentences himself.

God's holiness is honored. Our sin is punished ... and we are redeemed.

God does what we cannot do so we can be what we dare not dream: perfect before God."[99]

LINK TO YOUR LIFE

It's easy to look at verses about God's power and think He's too big, too powerful, too busy to bother. Yet that logic diametrically is in opposition to the character of God. God is both powerful and personal. There is nothing so small that God does not care about, nor is there anything too big God can't handle. We need to take to heart and apply the words of the apostle Paul:

> "And my God will meet all your needs according
> to the riches of his glory in Christ Jesus" (Philippians
> 4:19).

Is there something — anything — going on in your life right now in which you need help? God is more than capable to handle it and waiting for you to share your need. A.W. Tozer asks, "What does it mean to us, that God Almighty has all the power there is? It means that since God has the ability always to do anything He wills to do, then nothing is harder or easier with God. 'Hard' and 'easy' can't apply to God because God has all the power there is. Hard or easy applies to me."[100]

So don't put limitations on God. Talk to God and allow Him to work in your life.

SMALL GROUP DISCUSSION

If you were to compare God to a superhero, which one would he be? (You can use more than one!) Describe a 'God is powerful' moment in your life. Pray as a group that you would see and experience God's power.

KEY VERSE

"I will exalt you, my God the King; I will praise your name for ever and ever. Every day I will praise you and extol your name for ever and ever. Great is the Lord and most worthy of praise; his greatness no one can fathom" (Psalm 145:1-3).

PRAYER

"God, you are all-powerful, and I am not. Forgive me for times I've tried to control situations, thinking I was the only one who could handle it. I want to trust you with all things, big and small.

Continue your prayer:

Amen."

Twenty-seven
God Is ... ALL-KNOWING

There's a lot of money in the cover-up business. Each Halloween, consumers spend nearly 7 billion dollars on candy, decorations, and costumes, allowing children to pretend to be someone else. For adults who want to dress up a body part or two, the plastic surgery industry cashes in at 10 billion dollars a year. The cosmetics industry tops them all at 13 billion dollars a year. Three industries totaling 30 billion dollars — every year. For perspective, let's take just one billion. If we paid one dollar every second of every day, it would take 31 years, 259 days, 1 hour, 46 minutes, and 40 seconds to reach one billion. Now multiply that by 30. Clearly, from an economic standpoint, these industries have captured the hearts of many.

But there is great irony in the fact that while we try to cover things up — blotches, blemishes, or bruises — God sees everything. Proverb 5:21 is revealing: "For the Lord sees clearly what a man does, examining every path he takes (NLT)." God knows it all, so playing hide-and-seek with God is pointless. When Adam and Eve hid in the garden after eating the forbidden fruit (Genesis 3:8), God knew just where to find them, even though He asked, "Where are you?" God's "where are you" questions are really invitations for us to quit playing a game and fully reveal ourselves to Him.

The idea that God knows everything about us can be both encouraging and frightening. J.I. Packer explains: "To the Christian believer, knowledge of God's omniscience brings the assurance that he has not been forgotten, but is being and will be cared for according to God's promise. To anyone who is not a Christian, however, the truth of God's universal knowledge must bring dread, for it comes as a reminder that one cannot hide either oneself or one's sins from God's view."[101]

Of course, the latter holds true for believers when we attempt to hide our sin. We are ashamed, and so we cover it up. Instead, we need to acknowledge God's goodness and run toward God, not away from him.

KEY QUOTE

"To say, 'Of course God is omniscient and knows everything' makes no effect on me. I don't care whether God is 'omni' anything; but when by the reception of the Holy Spirit I begin to realize that God knows all the deepest possibilities there are in me, knows all the eccentricities of my being, I find that the mystery of myself is solved by this besetting God."[102] — Oswald Chambers

DYK . . .

Bible characters are inspiring. Sure, their courage and faith motivate me to put my trust in Jesus, but — honestly — I connect most with their failure. A.W. Tozer writes about Jacob's life:

> There was duplicity, there was dishonesty, there was greed. He cheated his own brother. He cheated his father. And he went on to cheat his father-in-law. Jacob seemed to be completely lacking in what we would call common honor. He showed a spirit of disloyalty and faithlessness in dealing with his brother and his father. . . .

I think we can safely say that the Jacob of those earlier years would have been voted the man least likely to get right with God. If we had been his judge and jury, we would have pronounced him hopeless. But of all those looking at Jacob, there was One who disagreed. That One was God. God, with His eternal omniscience, saw in Jacob something worthwhile.[103]

And God sees something worthwhile in you, too.

LINK TO YOUR LIFE

Take comfort, God is near. When you are afraid, remember that God is not just close by or next to you; God is holding you. Let that comfort produce courage as you step up to face your fear. Do you have unconfessed sin? You may have hidden it from family and friends, but it's impossible to hide it from God. God has not abandoned you. He is before you, waiting to help you. So take the next step and confess your sin to God.

And when you do, you get to take comfort, because God is near.

SMALL GROUP DISCUSSION

Do you like or dislike the fact that God knows everything? How does it comfort you, and how is it awkward? Since God knows everything . . . anything you need to confess? Pray silently as a group and then give one another a chance to share, if needed.

KEY VERSE

"God, investigate my life; get all the facts firsthand.

I'm an open book to you; even from a distance, you know what I'm thinking.

You know when I leave and when I get back; I'm never out of your sight.

You know everything I'm going to say before I start the first sentence.

I look behind me and you're there, then up ahead and you're there, too — your reassuring presence, coming and going.

This is too much, too wonderful — I can't take it all in!" (Psalm 139:1-6, The Message)

PRAYER

"God, I love verse 6 in Psalm 139: 'This is too much, too wonderful — I can't take it all in!' It's a reminder that you and your ways are unimaginable. You are too good, too powerful, too everything. Help me to seek to know you like you know me.

Continue your prayer:

Amen."

Twenty-eight
God Is . . . LISTENING

Traffic lights remind me of prayer. Green is go, yellow is slow, and red is no. I know, red means stop, but that would have killed my rhythm. The analogy makes sense, however. God does answer prayer — every one. They're just not always answered the way I want. When my prayer is selfish or unhealthy, God says no. When the timing of my prayer is off, God says "slow down," or tells me to wait. But when the timing and request are right, God says go with a green light.

Too simple for you? Guess what? It's that simple.

Prayer is a relationship, not a formula. There is no magical phrase, posture, or activity that will induce God to listen intently. Instead, God is listening, all the time, with great interest, and He is waiting to hear from you.

King David believed God was listening:

"When I called, you answered me; you greatly emboldened me" (Psalm 138:3).

"Lord my God, I called to you for help, and you healed me" (Psalm 30:2).

And Jesus further illustrates this in Matthew 7:

> "Ask and it will be given to you; seek and you will find; knock and the door will be opened to you. For everyone who asks receives; the one who seeks finds; and to the one who knocks, the door will be opened" (Matthew 7:7, 8).

The verses that follow show Jesus adding a bit of levity to the topic. After Jesus charges us to ask, seek, and knock, He raises an important question: who do you think God is? Whether you're a father or not, you know that a good father would never purposefully harm or deceive his child. If that's true about an earthly father, Jesus says, how much more would it be of a heavenly father who is pure, holy, and loving? That question is paramount. And, in fact, is the premise of this entire section of this book. Do we truly know who God is . . . or has our notion of God become corrupted?

God is a loving Father who is listening and answering our prayer in a manner consistent with His character. We may not get everything we ask for — and for that we should be thankful.

KEY QUOTE

PRAY, v. To ask that the laws of the universe be annulled in behalf of a single petitioner, confessedly unworthy.[104] — Ambrose Bierce, *The Devil's Dictionary*

DYK . . .

Too often our prayers are a one-way, rather than two-way, conversation. This is best illustrated in a story: "Helen Simonson, the mother of a religious family, was listening to her daughter Susanna saying a rather lengthy bedtime prayer. 'Dear God,' prayed the child, 'let me do well in my test tomorrow. Make my friends be nice to me. Tell my brother not to mess up my room. And please get my father to raise my allowance. And . . . ' The mother interrupted, 'Don't bother to give God instructions. Just report for duty.'"[105] God does hear us, but be sure to spend time in quiet so you can hear from God.

LINK TO YOUR LIFE

In a conference I recently attended, pastor and author Mark Batterson reminded me that when I pray, it's not my name at stake, it's God's. As a result, I should pray confidently because I don't have to worry about my reputation; instead, it's God who is on the line as to whether he'll come through. And when we pray, we're prone to pray ASAP (as soon as possible) prayers. We want to close our eyes and have the answer to our prayer before we open them. Instead, we ought to dig in and offer ALAIT (as long as it takes) prayers. This makes sense when we remember that God is not a slot machine who answers prayer based on random luck. Rather, He's a loving Father who responds with wisdom and in appropriate timing.

SMALL GROUP DISCUSSION

What's an answered prayer you continue to thank God for? What's a prayer you're still waiting for God to answer? Take time now to pray as a group.

KEY VERSE

"In my distress I called to the Lord; I cried to my God for help. From his temple he heard my voice; my cry came before him, into his ears" (Psalm 18:6).

PRAYER

"Thank you, Heavenly Father, that you hear my prayer and answer with love and wisdom. Continue to teach me about prayer, that I might grow in my knowledge and faith of you.

Continue your prayer:

Amen."

Twenty-nine
God Is a . . . A REFUGE

In C.S. Lewis' classic series *The Chronicles of Narnia*, we meet a lion named Aslan, the true ruler of Narnia. When Lucy, a young girl, learns that Aslan is a lion, she is frightened and asks, "Is he safe?" Mr. Beaver replies, "'Course he isn't safe. But he's good." A perfect description of the powerful and loving Aslan, who is but a metaphor for our Almighty God. God isn't safe. He will bring judgment upon the world with all-consuming power. But He is good. He invites us to be in relationship with Him, and welcomes us in any condition. In fact, God is so good that He illustrated His love in the supreme sacrifice of Jesus.

Psalm 46:1 says, "God is our refuge and strength, an ever-present help in trouble." The word *refuge* is used 20 times in the Bible to describe God. A refuge is a safe place to heal and renew, and it's also a fortification from which a counterattack can be launched. Other English words in the Bible that describe God include fortress, rock, shade, sheltering wings, shield, and tower.

Many people fear God, which is healthy and appropriate. But some take it too far and their fear prevents them from going to God when they've made wrong choices, or when they've been hurt by another. But the poets in Psalms and Proverbs and the prophets

Isaiah, Jeremiah, and Joel want us to know that God is a refuge we can run to, a secure tower who will protect us and shield us from an enemy.

Mr. Beaver wanted Lucy to understand the awesome power of Aslan, but she also needed to know his character. In the same way, run to God who welcomes you and heals you so that he can then use you in the lives of others. In the words of Charles Spurgeon, "The ark was a great ark, which held all kinds of creatures; and our Christ is a great Refuge, who saves all kinds of sinners."[106]

KEY QUOTE

"But the God of our fathers, who raised up this country to be the refuge and asylum of the oppressed and downtrodden of all nations, will not let it perish now. I may not live to see it . . . I do not expect to see it, but God will bring us through safe."[107] — Abraham Lincoln, weeks before the Battle of Gettysburg

DYK . . .

Horatio Spafford, the author of the hymn "It Is Well," wrote the lyrics while in extreme grief. In 1871, Spafford's son died, and months later, after investing heavily in real estate on the shore of Lake Michigan, he lost his family's financial savings when the buildings were destroyed in the Chicago Fire. Seeking solace for his wife and four daughters, he placed them on a ship to Europe, planning on meeting them in a few days. After being struck by another vessel, the ship sank in 12 minutes, with only his wife surviving. It was on the ship to meet his wife that he penned the words to the famous hymn.

"It is noteworthy, however, that Spafford does not dwell on the theme of life's sorrows and trials but focuses attention in the third stanza on the redemptive work of Christ and in the fourth verse anticipates His glorious second coming. Humanly speaking, it is amazing that one could experience such personal tragedies and sorrows as did Horatio Spafford and still be able to say with such convincing clarity, 'It is well with my soul.'"[108]

LINK TO YOUR LIFE

So what do you do when you feel depressed or beat up or alone?

- First, remind yourself repeatedly that you are not alone. Memorize Psalm 46:1, and recite it every time you doubt its truth.
- Second, talk to God about it. Pray or journal your thoughts and concerns.
- Next, sing to God about it. You don't have to write a song; instead, listen to worship songs so that you can keep your mind and spirit fixed on God and who He is. Our problems shrink when we focus on God.
- Finally, spend time with a friend. Share what's going on and ask your friend to pray for you. Do an activity with your friend to keep your mind and body busy.

SMALL GROUP DISCUSSION

Think back to a time you cried out to God for help. How did God answer you . . . or did he not? Is there a way you want or need God to be a refuge today? Share with the group.

KEY VERSE

"The Lord's voice will roar from Zion and thunder from Jerusalem, and the heavens and the earth will shake.

But the Lord will be a refuge for his people, a strong fortress for the people of Israel" (Joel 3:16, NLT).

PRAYER

"God, truths like this humble me and expand my view of you. Thank you for not only always being there, but for helping me heal and find renewed purpose.

Continue your prayer:

Amen."

Thirty
God Is ... APPROACHABLE

What do you do with your questions and doubts? If you're like most, you stuff them or sweep them under the rug. That's an unhealthy way to live, but it appears to be safer. But safer than what?

- We withhold our questions from God so that we don't disappoint him, yet God knows everything . . . including our doubts and questions.
- We withhold our questions from people at church so that we don't look foolish, but why are we more concerned with their approval than our own peace of mind?
- We withhold our questions from family and friends so that they won't worry, which only proves we believe the world revolves around us, and that we have little faith in our loved ones.

If only we had a biblical example of someone who doubted. Actually, the Bible is exploding with doubters, those who disbelieved that God would guide or provide. And time after time, God responds as a loving Father, not a vengeful foe. God is approachable.

I previously mentioned Job, and we discovered that despite his suffering, questioning, and doubting, God was with him. As a result, author Larry Richards says we can have "certainty that despite our suffering, God is our Friend, [and that] is perhaps the true message of Job."[109]

But let's look at the prophet Habakkuk. The book by that prophet's name is a short book that begs God for answers. "How long, O Lord, must I call for help? But you do not listen! 'Violence is everywhere!' I cry, but you do not come to save" (Habakkuk 1:2, 3, NLT). Ever feel like that? Alone, confused, and wondering why God doesn't flex some muscle to deal with challenging situations in our lives and in the world? Habakkuk felt that way and let God know it. His intense, honest prayer reveals his desire for an answer, and his trust that God was listening. Two writers summarize the book this way: "Habakkuk's book begins with an interrogation of God but ends as an intercession to God. Worry is transformed into worship. Fear turns to faith. Terror becomes trust. Hang-ups are resolved with hope. Anguish melts into adoration. . . . What begins with a question mark ends in an exclamation point. The answer to Habakkuk's 'Why?' is 'Who!' His confusion, 'Why all the conflict?' is resolved with his comprehension of who is in control: God!"[110]

God is big and able to defend himself, so we ought not worry about withholding our questions. Healthy relationships have a foundation of honesty that allows frank dialogue, so instead of being intimidated by being real, realize God is waiting to hear from you — and he wants to hear everything.

KEY QUOTE

"In story times, when the foundation of existence is shaken, when the moment trembles in fearful expectation of what may happen, when every explanation is silent at the sight of the wild uproar, when a man's heart groans in despair, and 'in bitterness of soul' he cries to heaven, then Job still walks at the side of the race and guarantees that there is a victory, guarantees that even if the individual loses in the strife, there is still God, who will still make its outcome such that we may be able to bear it; yea, more glorious than any human expectation."[111] — Soren Kierkegaard

DYK . . .

The best way to get answers to your questions is to get to know God. In *Bruce & Stan's Guide to God*, they offer the following recommendations:

- *Knowing God*, by J.I. Packer. Not an easy read, but one of the most rewarding.
- *Pleasing God*, authored by R.C. Sproul. We don't have a natural inclination to honor God, but this book will help.
- *Can Man Live Without God?*, by Ravi Zacharias. A philosophical argument against living as if there is no God.
- *The Fingerprint of God*, Hugh Ross. An astrophysicist explains recent scientific discoveries that point to the identity of the Creator.
- *Does It Matter If God Exists?*, by Millard J. Erickson. A veteran pastor helps us understand who God is and what he does for us.

LINK TO YOUR LIFE

When Satan tempted Jesus after His time in the wilderness (Matthew 4:1-12), Satan assumed Jesus' physical fatigue would produce doubt in the Savior. When he said, "If you are the Son of God . . . " Satan was trying to nurture any kernel of doubt that might have developed in Jesus' heart. Jesus responded quoting the Bible, solidifying His steadfast faith.

Author Larry Richards addresses the topic of doubt: "This is one temptation we are particularly susceptible to. When troubles come, we feel panic and uncertainty. We begin to doubt and to wonder if God is with us or not. Jesus reminds us that the way to triumph in such situations is not to demand God prove His presence, but simply to trust the love He has demonstrated so clearly. For us, that ultimate demonstration is in Christ's death and resurrection. Surely He who has given His own Son to redeem us will never leave or forsake His own."[112]

SMALL GROUP DISCUSSION

Talk about very real instances of doubt. Don't question people or make them feel small for their questions. Go first, and talk about some very real doubts you've had. Remember: God can handle it.

KEY VERSE

"Have mercy on me, Lord, for I am faint;
heal me, Lord, for my bones are in agony.
My soul is in deep anguish.
How long, Lord, how long?
Turn, Lord, and deliver me;
save me because of your unfailing love" (Psalm 6:2-4).

PRAYER

"God, thank you for being there for me, for inviting me to speak with you about anything. Help me trust you today and teach me to find answers in your Bible.

Continue your prayer:

Amen."

Thirty-one
God Is ... OUR FRIEND

We all know there's a clear distinction between a friend and an acquaintance. There's nothing wrong with being an acquaintance, but there are different expectations and privileges. Even among friends, there's a variance. There are those you'd go to the movies with and those you'd call in the middle of the night with a desperate need.

The same is true with God. He invites all of us to have a relationship with him, but his desire is that we would honor that relationship through a life of faith and action. Oswald Chambers writes, "Friendship with God is faith in action in relation to God and to our fellow men. I love others as God has loved me, and I see in the ingratitude of others the ingratitude which I have exhibited to God. The fellowship which arises out of such a friendship is a delight to the heart of God."[113]

The Apostle Paul writes a powerful truth in Romans 5:11 about our status with God:

> "So now we can rejoice in our wonderful new relationship with God because our Lord Jesus Christ has made us friends of God" (NLT).

Christ's work on the cross entitles us to be friends with God, but Jesus clarifies what this looks like in John 15 when He says, "You are my friends if you do what I command." We are to move beyond the movie-going type of friendship and be sacrificial servants. Abraham (James 2:23; 2 Chronicles 20:7; and Isaiah 41:8) was identified as a friend of God, and Bible teacher J. Carl Laney offers specific rationale:

> "Abraham's example provides believers with a pattern for knowing God intimately and obeying God willingly. I believe the order is significant. You are less inclined to obey someone you don't know. But if you know the person who gives you orders and you have confidence in his or her power, wisdom, and loving concern, you will be willing to obey that person's most challenging demands."[114]

Abraham believed God and obeyed him. Seems simple enough, but as Dr. Laney describes above, it's precipitated by a healthy relationship. This is, of course, true in our relationships with parents or other family members. When someone says "trust me," a foundation of trust already needs to have been established. And the best way for trust to develop is to spend time, lots of time, with a person. Our relationship with God is no different. In order to be comfortable trusting and obeying God, we need to develop a relationship with God, and that develops over time. We, however, are the direct beneficiaries because the more time we spend with God, the healthier lives we live. If you are a believer in Jesus, the Bible tells us God is your friend.

Are you God's acquaintance or friend?

KEY QUOTE

"A friend of God is not one who talks about God, but one who walks with God; and when people follow our walk and actions, they are apt to be disappointed. The greatest tribute a departed saint could have on his tombstone would be, 'He was a friend of God.' Abraham proved it with his actions, with the works of his faith."[115] — Spiros Zodhiates

DYK . . .

Jesus' offer of friendship has to be the most unequal friendship ever formed. Jesus is the eternal God-in-flesh, and we are desperate sinners in need of salvation. Greek scholar A.T. Robertson unpacks Jesus' statement "I have called you friends" by saying the Greek form of that statement (perfect active indicative) means it describes a permanent state of new dignity. To that I say: wow.

LINK TO YOUR LIFE

Being a friend of God means more than simply gaining knowledge about him. But that is important too. Do you have a regular time set aside to read your Bible and pray? If not, that's the perfect first step. And you're more likely to have success if you do this with a friend. You don't have to do it side by side, but have an accountability relationship with someone to help keep you on track. The biggest challenge — and the most rewarding one — will be to follow through on what you learn from your time with God. This is critical because it establishes a pattern of trust. Is God trustworthy? Will it really be beneficial to obey what God commands? Go ahead: Find out!

SMALL GROUP DISCUSSION

Talk about the times you've felt God was close, just like a friend. Talk about times he felt like anything but. What was different in the circumstances? In the outcome? What did you learn?

KEY VERSE

"You are my friends if you do what I command. I no longer call you servants, because a servant does not know his master's business. Instead, I have called you friends, for everything that I learned from my Father I have made known to you" (John 15:14, 15).

PRAYER

"Heavenly Father, I don't want there to be any doubt that I am your friend. I want to live in such a way that it is clear that I am friends with God.

Continue your prayer:

Amen."

Thirty-two
God Is ... JEALOUS

God is jealous? How can God be good if He's jealous? It's an important question , one requiring a clear distinction between two types of jealousy. Author J.I. Packer describes these as "vicious jealousy" and "zealous jealousy." The first is the kind with which we're most familiar. Vicious jealousy is destructive. It expresses itself with clear, loud declarations of "I want what you have," and visible expressions of "I will hate you until I have what you have." Not exactly a warm, fuzzy way to live. Conversely, zealous jealousy is healthy. It is protective and watchful. It is a deep conviction and commitment to protect the honor and welfare of another. God is jealous in this way.

So what makes God jealous? God is jealous anytime we put items or individuals before Him, when we begin to worship the created rather than the Creator. In Deuteronomy 32:21 God cries out, "They made me jealous by what is no god and angered me with their worthless idols." We are God's creation, and we belong to Him. In fact, according to Psalm 24:1, everything belongs to Him: "The earth is the Lord's, and everything in it, the world, and all who live in it." God wants and deserves our complete devotion, and when he doesn't get it, he is jealous for it. In short, according to Wayne Grudem, "God's jealousy means that God continually seeks to protect his own honor."[116]

Still, some might think God is being petty, a bit too controlling. We're tempted to think along those lines only when we fail to understand that we have been purchased at a great price, the life of Jesus Christ. As a result, we should begin to develop or pray for a zeal for God that produces a hunger for him. Because God's concern for us is so great, we ought to reciprocate. Bishop J.C. Ryle says, "Zeal in religion is a burning desire to please God. A zealous man in religion is pre-eminently a man of one thing."

I struggle with putting many things before God. I want to be a man of one thing: God Almighty.

KEY QUOTE

"God's jealousy is not a compound of frustration, envy and spite, as human jealousy so often is, but appears instead as a [literally] praiseworthy zeal to preserve something supremely precious."[117]
— J.I. Packer

DYK ...

Norm Geisler describes God's jealousy: "Foremost among these [God's attributes] is God's holiness; God is particularly jealous about preserving His own uniqueness. Of course, all of God's attributes are unique and comprise the one infinite, absolutely perfect, and supreme God. The theological argument for God's jealousy can be formulated as follows:

1) God is unique and supreme.
2) God is holy, loving, and morally perfect.
3) Hence, God is uniquely and supremely holy, loving, and morally perfect.
4) Whatever is supremely holy, loving, and perfect is to be preserved with the utmost zeal.
5) God's jealousy is His zeal to preserve His own holy supremacy.
6) Therefore, He is eminently justified in His jealousy. Indeed,

it is essential to His very nature: His name is Jealous (Ex. 34:14)."[118]

LINK TO YOUR LIFE

God's jealousy should not intimidate us because Romans 5:1 reminds us we now have peace with God through Jesus Christ. However, a healthy fear of God would benefit us all. Take time to evaluate your life this week. Pray, talk to others, and evaluate how you use your time. Is anyone or anything consuming your attention more than it should? Is God jealous for your love and your life? Say yes to God this week more than you normally would.

SMALL GROUP DISCUSSION

Talk about jealousy you have seen, or lived yourself, that has really hurt people. (Do not use names or identities.) Now contrast that jealousy with what you know of the proper jealousy that is part of God's character.

KEY VERSE

"I will rescue you for my sake — yes, for my own sake! I will not let my reputation be tarnished, and I will not share my glory with idols!" (Isaiah 48:11, NLT)

PRAYER

"God, thank you for your jealousy. It reveals your continued love for me. Give me a zeal for following you that is unlike any I've had before.

Continue your prayer:

Amen."

SECTION 3: Jesus is . . .

Thirty-three
Jesus Is ... GOD

The statement "Jesus is God" is a game-changer.

Strip Jesus of his deity, and he's a tame, manageable religious figure. He's a good man, even a dynamic teacher. But the moment you acknowledge Jesus is God in the flesh, eternity is altered. Jesus moves from holiday figurine to the only One who offers forgiveness for our past, courage for our present, and hope for our future. But saying "Jesus is God" doesn't prove a thing. Many throughout history have made similar claims about their own — or another's — deity.

What makes the "Jesus is God" claim unique?

Believers' Claims

The Bible is filled with believers claiming Jesus is God. John 1:1 says, "In the beginning was the Word, and the Word was with God, and the Word was God" (John 1:1). Verses 14 and following identify the Word as Jesus Christ. In Colossians 1:15, Paul calls Jesus "the image of the invisible God." Need a profile picture of God? Look to Jesus. In the following chapter (Colossians 2:9), Paul writes that "in Christ lives all the fullness of God in a human body." More verses: Titus 2:13 and Romans 9:5.

Jesus' Own Claims

Some assert that Jesus had fanatical followers who so longed for a savior that they would say anything to convince themselves and others that Jesus was the One. Blind allegiance does motivate people to say and do crazy things, but the disciples died for what they believed. They could have easily denied their faith to save their lives, but then they would have denied the truth. Regardless, it's important to evaluate how Jesus responded to others' claims of his deity. If the claims were not true, certainly Jesus could have cleared things up. What we find, however, is that Jesus not only affirmed those statements, he made bold declarations himself.

When Jesus' identity was in question, He attempted to clarify things in John 8:58 when He said, "I tell you the truth, before Abraham was even born, I Am!" Those who heard this were astounded. Bruce Barton writes, "Abraham, as with all human beings, had come into existence at one point in time. But Jesus never had a beginning — he was eternal and therefore God. This ["I Am"] statement may refer to Exodus 3:14, in which God unveiled his identity to Moses with the name 'I am who I am,' and to Isaiah 45:18, 'I am the LORD, and there is no other.' Thus, Jesus was claiming to be God."[119] The Jews recognized that Jesus claimed to be God because they wanted to stone him for blasphemy, according to the law found in Leviticus 24:16.

In John 10:27-33, Jesus identifies himself as equal with God, and again the Jews pick up stones. When Jesus seeks an explanation for their attempts on his life they reply, "We are not stoning you for any good work but for blasphemy, because you, a mere man, claim to be God." Jesus did not correct any misunderstanding. He is God.

Jesus' Demonstrations of Deity

It's one thing to declare your deity and have others affirm that claim, but declarations are just words. Proof is required to support such uninhibited utterances. Consider the following examples:

#1 — Jesus forgives sin

In Mark 2:5, Jesus said to a paralyzed man, "Son, your sins are forgiven." Immediately Jesus' statement was challenged: "Why does this fellow talk like that? He's blaspheming! Who can forgive sins but God alone?" (Mark 2:7). Jesus claimed that he could forgive sins, something reserved only for God.

#2 — Jesus allows other to worship him

The first commandment says we are to have no other gods before God. Yet the Bible describes many who worshipped Jesus, and Jesus accepted it. One example is found in John 20:28, when Thomas worships Jesus and is affirmed for it.

#3 — Jesus redefines the Sabbath

John 5:16-18 describes how Jesus changed the rules for the Sabbath, an action reserved only for God.

The Bible claims that Jesus is God. People may choose to disregard what the Bible says, but they cannot say the Bible is silent on the subject.

KEY QUOTE

"Alexander, Caesar, Charlemagne, and I myself have founded great empires. . . . But Jesus alone founded His empire upon love, and to this very day, millions would die for Him. Jesus Christ was more than a man."[120] — Napoleon Bonaparte

DYK . . .

If Jesus is not God, neither salvation nor Christianity exists. Theologian Wayne Grudem identifies three reasons it is crucial to acknowledge Christ's deity:

　　1) Only someone who is infinite God could bear the full penalty for all the sins of all those who would believe in him — any

finite creature would have been incapable of bearing that penalty;

2) Salvation is from the Lord, and the whole message of Scripture is designed to show that no human being, no creature, could ever save man — only God himself could; and

3) Only someone who was truly and fully God could be the one mediator between God and man (1 Timothy 2:5), both to bring us back to God and also to reveal God most fully to us (John 14:9).[121]

LINK TO YOUR LIFE

Believing Jesus is God is foundational to the Christian faith. Bible teacher Max Anders identifies key consequences to not doing so: "If you don't believe Jesus is God . . .

1) You must admit that the Bible is full of lies.

2) Jesus is not who he said he is, and he can offer you no hope for this life or the next.

3) There is no such thing as right or wrong. You can do whatever society will let you get away with. And so can everyone else."[122]

SMALL GROUP DISCUSSION

If you polled 100 people at a college or supermarket, how many would believe that Jesus is God? Why do you think that it? Discuss what you identify as the most interesting point from this chapter.

KEY VERSE

"Abraham, Isaac, and Jacob are their ancestors, and Christ himself was an Israelite as far as his human nature is concerned. And he is God, the one who rules over everything and is worthy of eternal praise! Amen" (Romans 9:5, NLT).

PRAYER

"Jesus, it is appropriate to worship you. You are deserving of my praise, adoration, and obedience.

Continue your prayer:

Amen."

Thirty-four
Jesus Is ... MAN

While some would argue Jesus' divinity, it's vital not to lose sight of the value of His humanity. The last chapter revealed Jesus as God, and this chapter identifies his human qualities, along with reasons his humanity matters.

Jesus possessed human qualities

Physically, he was hungry (Matthew 4:2), thirsty (John 19;28), and got tired (Mark 4:38). Emotionally, Jesus demonstrated sorrow (Matthew 26:38), anger and grief (Mark 3:5), compassion (Mark 1:41), and was tempted to sin (Hebrews 4:15).

Jesus was led by the Holy Spirit

Jesus showed us how to live, and in the Gospel of John we receive a powerful challenge: "Those who say they live in God should live their lives as Jesus did" (1 John 2:6, NLT). While we won't attain Jesus' standard of perfection, He did model a Spirit-filled life. Clinton Arnold writes, "In Jesus, we see what it looks like to live and move through this world fully empowered by the Spirit of God. This includes Jesus' example of how to resist temptation."[123] When Jesus was temped in the wilderness, Luke writes that Jesus was full of the Holy Spirit and fought temptation with the Word of God — a great example for us.

Jesus acted as our substitute

The writer of Hebrews clearly states why Jesus had to be human.

> We also know that the Son did not come to help angels; he came to help the descendants of Abraham. Therefore, it was necessary for him to be made in every respect like us, his brothers and sisters, so that he could be our merciful and faithful High Priest before God. Then he could offer a sacrifice that would take away the sins of the people (Hebrews 2:16, 17, NLT).

If Jesus had not been human, he could not have died in our place in order to pay the penalty of our sins. We needed a perfect sacrifice — a substitute — and Jesus was the only one who could do it.

Jesus understands us

We'll address this more in chapter 37, but the fact that God became a man reveals that God understands what it means to be human. Jesus was tempted in every way that we are, and because he has promised to always be with us (Matthew 28:20), we can be confident that he will provide all we need, whenever we need.

KEY QUOTE

"Jesus was not an angel, a bodiless manifestation of God, or the Spirit of God coming on a human being for a period of time. Jesus is God who became fully human."[124] — Clinton Arnold

DYK . . .

The Nicene Creed (325 AD) recognizes the foundational

biblical teaching that Jesus Christ was 100 percent God and 100 percent man. Any false teaching about Jesus' life denies one or both of those truths.

One heresy was called Docetism. It taught that Jesus was God but only "seemed" to be human. Instead, Docetists believed Jesus was a phantom. They were convinced God could not suffer; therefore, Jesus only looked like he was suffering. Norm Geisler identifies several reasons this view was rejected by the early Christians: "If this is so, then Christ was not really tempted as we are and did not really die because a spirit can do neither of these things. Hence, He was not really 'one of us' and cannot be our substitute in atoning for our sins. Also, His resurrection was nothing more than a return to His natural state, and it has no implications for us as to our future."[125]

LINK TO YOUR LIFE

The humanity of Jesus is a vital component to the Christian faith. Yes, Jesus' life and death provide forgiveness for our sin and the opportunity for an eternal relationship with God. But that's not all. The fact that Jesus became fully human:

- changes how I pray (I know that he can relate to me and understand me)
- helps me when I face temptation (I know that he dealt with it, too)
- consoles me when I am down, (I know he faced great disappointments)
- strengthens me when I feel weak (I know he experienced sickness and the limitations of bodily existence).[126]

SMALL GROUP DISCUSSION

If Jesus were both fully God and fully man . . . talk about the implications. What does each part mean to you? What does it mean if both are equally true?

KEY VERSES

"So the Word became human and made his home among us" (John 1:14, NLT).

"And Jesus grew in wisdom and stature, and in favor with God and man" (Luke 2:52).

PRAYER

"Jesus, you voluntarily gave up your privileges of deity in order to sacrificially give up your life so that we can have an eternal relationship with you. Help me never tire in showing my gratitude.

Continue your prayer:

Amen."

Thirty-five
Jesus Is . . . FORGIVING

I love seeing older people give their lives to God. I prefer seeing young people do it, knowing they have many years to continue to grow in faith and be used by God. But there's something special hearing an older man or woman finally give in to God's love.

Mr. Donado wanted nothing to do with God and was frustrated that his daughter asked "the pastor" to visit. "I don't need no pastor, and I don't need no God!" he shouted loud enough for me to hear from the front door. At least I knew where to begin the conversation. "Hi, Mr. Donado," I tried to say confidently. "Sounds like you're excited to see me." Mr. Donado ignored me for a few minutes, but I assured him I was not there to convert him or make him to do anything he didn't want to do. In fact, I promised I'd leave if he'd let me read some Bible verses and ask a few questions. "Let's get it done then," he said with his back to me. "And don't bother taking off your coat!" "Too late," I shot back, wondering why I didn't withhold the sarcasm. "But I promise I won't ask for something to drink. Fair enough?" My question was met with silence, so I opened my Bible.

I shared two Bible stories with Mr. Donado. I read from John 8, when Jesus forgives the woman caught in the act of adultery.

And I read Luke 23, when Jesus tells the criminal hanging on the cross beside Him, "Truly I tell you, today you will be with me in paradise" (Luke 23:43, NIV). There are many stories I could have read describing Jesus' acts of forgiveness, but those are a couple of my favorites. Those stories comfort the souls of imperfect people — I'm certain that's why I like them. I love Philip Ryken's quote that there is divine love in the forgiveness of Jesus. Jesus forgives everyone, so why wouldn't he forgive me? There is no reason, other than our own resistance. I'm happy to say, Mr. Donado's rock solid exterior did have a crack, big enough to believe Jesus' forgiveness was for him, too.

Have you received Jesus' forgiveness? Now is the perfect time to share an experience Mr. Donado had years ago. There's no magic formula — just let Jesus know you give up trying to be perfect and that you want his forgiveness for your past and leadership for your future. And if you're already a believer but have given up on some family members or friends, take heart from Mr. Donado's words to me and his daughters before I left: "Thanks for stopping by, and thanks for not giving up on me."

KEY QUOTE

"It is an unspeakable miracle of divine grace that crimson sins can be made whiter than snow. I can empathize with the man who chose one word for his tombstone — FORGIVEN. And also with the Irishman who said, 'The Lord Jesus has forgiven me all my sins, and he's never going to hear the end of it.'"[127] — William MacDonald

DYK...

"The annually repeated sacrifices of the Old Testament were unable to perfect the worshipers; by contrast, through a single offering of himself, Jesus forgives and perfects forever the ones being sanctified."[128] Christians all too often ignore the "forgive and perfect" portion of Jesus' forgiveness. Instead, we are prone to become depressed, overwhelmed by feelings of guilt.

Well, I've got good news: Jesus not only forgives, he washes away our guilt. Stand tall on what Jesus has done. Don't be buried by what you've done.

LINK TO YOUR LIFE

Our lives must provide evidence for all that Jesus forgives today and every day. Live like you are forgiven. Forgive like you've been forgiven.

SMALL GROUP DISCUSSION

Open up with your group about where you have felt the forgiveness of Jesus, and the impact it's had on your life. Start the sharing with your own story; it's likely a number of others will follow.

KEY VERSE

"'The Lord is compassionate and merciful, slow to get angry and filled with unfailing love.

He will not constantly accuse us, nor remain angry forever.

He does not punish us for all our sins; he does not deal harshly with us, as we deserve.

For his unfailing love toward those who fear him is as great as the height of the heavens above the earth" (Psalm 103:8-11, NLT).

PRAYER

"Jesus, may I never tire of reflecting on and sharing with others what you have done for me. Thank you for your forgiveness. Thank you. Thank you. Thank you.

Continue your prayer:

Amen."

Thirty-six
Jesus Is … DEMANDING

There's a story about a church that hosted an event featuring "the world's smartest horse." The horse was asked how many commandments were in the Bible, and it stomped its hoof ten times. Then the horse was asked for the number of Jesus' disciples, and it stomped twelve times. A man stood up from the back and asked, "How many hypocrites are in this church?" The horse tap-danced on all fours.

We can laugh at the story but ought to cry at the indictment. Author Thomas Russell Ybarra takes a shot at believers when he writes:

> A Christian is a man who feels
> Repentance on a Sunday
> For what he did on Saturday
> And is going to do on Monday.[129]

People outside the church demand more from believers, and whether that's fair or not, Jesus was quite demanding himself. His invitation to "follow me" was about more than taking a walk; it was about changing our lives. And while Jesus befriended sinners, he had no mercy for religious hypocrisy. In fact, when dealing with negligent religious leaders, his "nice guy" persona took a hit. In Matthew 23, Jesus addresses irresponsible teachers of the law, those who were more focused on winning approval from man than God. They were meticulous about their reputations while allowing their spiritual bodies to decay. In response, Jesus calls them hypocrites, blind guides, blind fools, blind men, whitewashed tombs, snakes, a brood of vipers, and said they were going to hell. Wow. Pretty strong. William Shakespeare captures the idea in Hamlet when he writes, "One may smile, and smile, and be a villain."

Jesus did not have a chip on his shoulder who wielded power in a careless manner. Rather, he demanded that those espousing faith live it with sincerity, especially those in leadership. In the book of James, a similar warning is offered, "Not many of you should become teachers, my fellow believers, because you know that we who teach will be judged more strictly" (James 3:1). And Jesus is not looking for perfection, either. Jesus demands authenticity, wanting our "yes to be yes" and our "no to be no."

How's your faith these days? If it's not doing well, there is a solution. Talk to God and some trustworthy friends about it. Ask your friends for prayer and support. That kind of humility honors God and authenticates your faith. Is your faith healthy? Celebrate and thank God! And continue to walk in the wisdom of the prophet Micah: "Do what is right, love mercy, and walk humbly with your God" (Micah 6:8, NLT).

KEY QUOTE

"For neither Man nor Angel can discern hypocrisy, the only evil that walks invisible, except to God alone." — John Milton, *Paradise Lost*

DYK . . .

We get our English word *hypocrite* from the Greek language. It literally means play actor, counterfeit, or one who speaks or acts under a feigned character. So Greek actors were called hypocrites.

LINK TO YOUR LIFE

Do you ever condemn people for the same sins you commit yourself? Instead, let others' sins motivate you to pray for them while reminding you of your own need for life change. Are you guilty of privately lowering God's standards in order to feel successful in your faith? Instead, humble yourself before God, acknowledging your need for Him on a daily basis. Spend time confessing any hypocrisy that is evident in your life and ask God for help in overcoming temptation today. (Don't worry about tomorrow.)

SMALL GROUP DISCUSSION

Explain why you agree or disagree with the following: God has unrealistic expectations for us. Have you ever felt overwhelmed with the expectation of living a perfect life? Explain why you think that's a healthy or unhealthy burden.

KEY VERSE

"In the same way, on the outside you appear to people as righteous but on the inside you are full of hypocrisy and wickedness" (Matthew 23:28).

PRAYER

"Heavenly Father, I want to live in a way that allows you to say, 'Well done, good and faithful servant.' Reveal any sin in my life and help me take the next steps in overcoming it.

Continue your prayer:

Amen."

Thirty-seven
Jesus Is ... UNDERSTANDING

Jesus understands what we're going through because he's been there, done that. Actually, he's been there and *didn't* do that, which is the significance of a relationship with Jesus. He is God, yet he's not distant because he understands everything you and I experience. Max Lucado writes, "Lust wooed him. Greed lured him. Power called him. Jesus — the human — was tempted. But Jesus — the holy God — resisted."[130]

Chuck Swindoll offers additional insight:

> As an adult, Jesus experienced as difficult a life as anyone could imagine. He knew poverty, temptation, and persecution, and He grew up in an occupied and oppressed nation. He knew all the pain we could possibly experience, and He died as the innocent victim of a violent mob after being falsely accused by His enemies and abandoned by His friends."[131]

The "Four Yorkshiremen" is a classic Monty Python skit

parodying four friends who reminisce about the olden days. Each friend attempts to outdo one another, exaggerating his difficult childhood, hoping to secure comfort from the others. While the sketch provides plenty of laughs, it reveals that it is impossible to truly understand another person's life. And while that may be true in human interaction, it is incorrect in our relationship with God. Jesus knows exactly what we're going through. He has been there.

Hebrews 2:18 provides good news: "Since he himself [Jesus] has gone through suffering and testing, he is able to help us when we are being tested" (NLT). As a result, we can take great comfort knowing that we are not alone, even when we feel that way. During the season of my life when I struggled with depression, I found it difficult to be around people — not a good time to be a pastor! But I was able to cling to the truth that Jesus knew how it felt to be alone and misunderstood. Even when I had difficulty verbalizing my prayers, I knew Jesus was with me, and that knowledge empowered me to make it through each day.

Regardless of what you're feeling or experiencing today, you are not alone. Jesus understands your situation and wants to help. More than that, he's prepared to carry you through it.

In fact, he's doing that now.

KEY QUOTE

"It is an extraordinary display of God's love for us that He would become human so that He could better understand us, sympathize with us, and know how to help us. Far from being a god who turns his head in horror when he sees us in our sin, our God reaches out to us and takes us by the hand to cleanse us and help us."[132] — Clinton Arnold

DYK . . .

When addressing Hebrews 4:15, a verse which says that Jesus was tempted in every way, one commentator writes, "This phrase does not mean that Christ underwent every single human temptation that is possible to experience in our day, but that He experienced in every way the full force of our temptation yet without yielding to it."[133]

LINK TO YOUR LIFE

"A little girl dressed in dungarees walked into a pet shop and asked whether they had a puppy with a lame leg. She had a dollar with which she wanted to buy it. The salesperson of the pet shop was surprised that the little girl wanted to buy a lame puppy. She asked, 'Why, don't you want to buy a puppy that can run around and play?' 'No, I want a lame one.' Finally, she pulled up one leg of her dungarees and showed her brace, saying, 'I don't walk so good, either.'"[134]

Feel alone? Rejected? Bitter? Misunderstood? Mistreated? Hopeless? Bring those feelings and the experiences that led to them to Jesus. Today. Don't think no one knows or cares what's going on in your life, because Jesus cares. And He already knows. So take time right now to pray, asking for God's direction and wisdom on what next step to take. Then take that step.

SMALL GROUP DISCUSSION

Share about a time you felt isolated and alone. Share about a deep pit of disappointment or depression. Explain why you think God could or could not have related to those feelings.

KEY VERSE

"*For we do not have a high priest who is unable to empathize with our weaknesses, but we have one who has been tempted in every way, just as we are — yet he did not sin*" (Hebrews 4:15).

PRAYER

"Jesus, just when I think I know you, my understanding of your power, might, and care increases exponentially. Thank you for knowing me and not rejecting me.

Continue your prayer:

Amen."

Thirty-eight
Jesus Is ... THE ONLY WAY TO GOD

Walter Kaiser correctly states that, "John 14:6 is one of those verses that are difficult not because we do not understand them, but because we understand them all too well."[135] So true! Many are offended by the title of this chapter, but it's important to note that it's a paraphrase of John 14:6, where Jesus says, "No one comes to the Father except through Me." Christians did not create this teaching with hopes to exclude anyone. It's Jesus' teaching and is both incredibly gracious and exceedingly welcoming.

God's graciousness is revealed in the fact that Jesus is the only one qualified to pay the penalty for our sin. His resume includes being sinless and divine. Impressive. What's also impressive is the penalty for our sin. Only Jesus is able to pay that penalty, and so in declaring that he is the only way, Jesus graciously clarifies for all how to respond to their sin problem.

My daughters were each born with varying degrees of jaundice. It's a liver disorder that causes the whites of a child's eyes and their skin to turn yellow. Untreated, it can be fatal. But fortunately, there is an easy cure for it. All that's required is to put the baby under a special light. The skin absorbs this light and it stimulates the liver to function properly. That's what we did with our children.

We could have responded by saying, "Wait a minute! That's sounds too easy! Put her under a light? How about we scrub her with soap and dip her in bleach? I'm sure if we scrub hard enough, we could get her skin coloring back to its normal self." The doctor would have said, "You don't understand. There is only one way to cure jaundice." We could have replied, "I don't like this one-way thing. How about we just ignore it and pretend that everything's OK?" The doctor would plead with us to trust her based upon her credentials.

Jesus is saying the same thing. His credentials prove his credibility. Not only is Jesus' statement gracious, it's also welcoming. Some are surprised by that, thinking Jesus is making a rather exclusive statement. I loved the way author Lee Strobel addressed this topic when speaking at a church. He said:

"Picture it this way. Suppose there are two popular vacation spots just out of town. One spot represents every other religious system that we've ever heard of. And this vacation place says, 'If you want to come in, if you want to have a membership, you have to pay for that membership.

· You have to achieve a certain level of spirituality.
· You have to perform a certain number of religious rituals.
· You have to accomplish a certain number of good deeds and then maybe we will let you in.'

That's what every other religion I've ever seen essentially says.

Christianity is different. Christianity is like a country club with the doors wide open: 'You want in, come on in.

· You don't have to buy your membership. Jesus Christ has already bought and paid for it with His death on the cross.
· Coming into our country club is not based on your qualifications. It's based on your acceptance of Jesus' invitation.
· The doors are open. I don't care if you're rich or poor.
· I don't care about the color of your skin.
· I don't care about where you're from.

· I don't care what your age is.

You decide if you want to come join our vacation club. It is your decision. But I'm going to keep the doors open. I'm going to keep them open because I really hope that you will come in and experience what we experience."'[136]

That is what Christianity is about. It is full of grace and available to all.

KEY QUOTE

"The gospel applies to all who believe in Jesus. God does not say that he will save those who climb mountains or clean up their addictions or relieve poverty or reach some designated level of goodness. He saves those who simply believe in Jesus as their Savior (John 3:16)."[137] — Bryan Chapell

DYK...

There are many different views of who can and cannot have a relationship with God.

1. Some say God gives salvation to everyone, no matter what. But in Matthew 25:41, Jesus says to a group of people, "Depart from me into the eternal fire prepared for the devil and his angels."
2. Others say God gives salvation to everyone except those who have committed the most atrocious sins. But in Titus 3:5 and Ephesians 2:8, 9, Paul reminds us that we are not saved by any effort on our part. Instead, we are saved because of God's mercy. Salvation is available to all.
3. Still others believe that sincere seekers will find salvation in God, regardless of what they believe. But this notion is the very one Paul countered when speaking to a group of religious people in Acts 17:22-31. (It's a passage worth reading and digesting.) It does matter what you believe.
4. A final group claims that only Jesus provides access to a

relationship with God — and that is the one position with ample biblical support (John 14:6; Acts 4:12).

All four positions cannot be true because they contradict one another. We are forced to decide whether we choose to believe what the Bible teaches.

LINK TO YOUR LIFE

Walter Kaiser offers a direct link to life: "If, then, this claim is true, two conclusions follow. First, we are deceiving ourselves if we think that we can come to God any other way than through Jesus. What is more, no other way will supplement or add to Jesus as the way. Second, if we are already following Jesus, we are called, in John's terms, to be witnesses to the truth and life found in Jesus."[138]

SMALL GROUP DISCUSSION

Why do you think people struggle with the thought that the only way to get to heaven is through Jesus? Have you? Is it possible that it's not an exclusive position at all, but an inclusive one? Talk about how they might be.

KEY VERSE

"Salvation is found in no one else, for there is no other name under heaven given to mankind by which we must be saved" (Acts 4:12).

PRAYER

"Heavenly Father, you did not have to provide a way for us to have a relationship with you. Thank you for your gift of Jesus.

Continue your prayer:

Amen."

Thirty-nine
Jesus Is . . . RESURRECTED

The comedian and filmmaker Woody Allen once said, "I don't want to achieve immortality through my work. I want to achieve it by not dying." Noble aspiration, but every last one of us will die. Even Jesus died . . . for a few days. The fact that Jesus rose from the dead ought to end the conversation on whether or not he's God. Here's a good rule for living: if a man walks out of his own grave, we ought to pay attention to everything he says.

Years ago, a rabbi who recognized the historicity of Jesus' resurrection was quoted in *Time* magazine. In response to a colleague's disbelief, the rabbi said, "[His] logic escapes me. He believes it is a possibility that Jesus was resurrected by God. At the same time he does not accept Jesus as the Messiah. But Jesus said that He was the Messiah. Why would God resurrect a liar?"[139] Fair question. Here are three of the most popular theories for rejecting the resurrection.

1) **The Swoon Theory** (the belief that Jesus did not die; he only fainted)

J. N. D. Anderson remarks on the hypothesis that Jesus did not die:

"Well . . . it's very ingenious. But it won't stand up to investigation. To begin with, steps were taken — it seems — to make quite sure that Jesus was dead; that surely is the meaning of the spear-thrust in His side. But suppose for argument's sake that He was not quite dead. Do you really believe that lying for hour after hour with no medical attention in a rock-hewn tomb in Palestine at Easter, when it's quite cold at night, would so far have revived Him, instead of proving the inevitable end to His flickering life, that He would have been able to loose Himself from yards of graveclothes weighted with pounds of spices, roll away a stone that three women felt incapable of tackling, and walk miles on wounded feet?"[140]

And don't forget Jesus would also have had to deal with the Roman guards protecting the tomb. Writing in the early 1900s, George Hanson said, "It is hard to believe that this was the favorite explanation of eighteenth-century rationalism."[141] This once-popular theory had such little evidence that its hypothesis is now obsolete.

2) **The Theft Theory** (the belief that the disciples came during the night and stole the body)

The Gospel of Matthew records this as the prevailing theory of its day. Yet writing from the 4th century AD, John Chrysostom acknowledges the fallacy of this theory: "For indeed even this establishes the resurrection, the fact I mean of their saying, that the disciples stole Him. For this is the language of men confessing, that the body was not there."[142]

The empty tomb can only be explained two ways:

1) It was a divine work or

2) It was a human work. But Jesus' enemies had no motive.

Quite the opposite, actually. They *wanted* the body to be there. And Jesus' friends had no power to accomplish such a feat. How could a group of fishermen — frightened enough to flee from the cross only two days before—get past trained Roman guards? If the disciples stole the body, why would they later be willing to die as martyrs for a story they knew to be a lie? And if Jesus' dead body was stolen, how could Jesus' resurrection appearances be explained?

Regarding this and other theories, George Hanson writes, "The simple faith of the Christian who believes in the Resurrection is nothing compared to the credulity of the skeptic who will accept the wildest and most improbable romances rather than admit the plain witness of historical certainties. *The difficulties of belief may be great; the absurdities of unbelief are greater.*"[143]

3) **The Wrong Tomb Theory** (the belief that the disciples found the tomb empty because they went to the wrong tomb)

While none of the theories are particularly credible, this is the easiest to dismiss. Numerous Bible passages indicate the disciples and women who went to Jesus' tomb knew the correct location. Plus, this was a private burial ground, not a public cemetery. And why would the Romans have placed guards at the wrong tomb? Finally, if the disciples went to the wrong tomb, why didn't the Jewish leaders take people to the correct tomb? Instead, they circulated a story that the disciples stole the body.

Years ago, author Josh McDowell sought to disprove Christianity. He knew proving the resurrection to be false would seal the deal. McDowell believed that Jesus' resurrection was one of two things:

1) the most wicked, vicious, heartless hoax ever presented or
2) the most amazing fact of history.

The result? "After more than seven hundred hours of studying this subject and thoroughly investigating its foundation, I can come to only one conclusion: The resurrection of Jesus Christ is not a heartless hoax; it is the most amazing fact of history! That is why the affirmation you will hear in many churches today is more than just a religious liturgy. It is a reliable historical fact: He is risen! He is risen indeed!"[144]

KEY QUOTE

"The evidence for Jesus' resurrection is so strong that nobody would question it except for two things: First, it is a very unusual event. And second, if you believe it happened, you have to change the way you live."[145] — Wolfhart Pannenberg

DYK . . .

If our hope in Christ is only for this life, we are to be pitied more than anyone in the world. That's an exact quote from the apostle Paul in 1 Corinthians 15:19. He recognizes that we are basing our entire faith on Jesus' resurrection, his defeat of death, and his demolition of the power of sin. The resurrection is more than an Easter story. It is indispensable to our faith. As Josh McDowell says, "The resurrection of Jesus Christ and Christianity stand or fall together."[146]

LINK TO YOUR LIFE

If you're at the end of your rope, you're still in good shape. You + Jesus = victory every time. "We are not to be surprised if living as Christians brings us to the place where we find we are at the end of our own resources, and that we are called to rely on the God who raises the dead."[147] — N.T.Wright

SMALL GROUP DISCUSSION

Why do you think people struggle with believing that Jesus walked out of his own tomb? Could the reasons be deeper than just struggling with various theories? If Jesus was resurrected from his grave, what are the implications for your life?

KEY VERSE

"For what I received I passed on to you as of first importance: that Christ died for our sins according to the Scriptures, that he was buried, that he was raised on the third day according to the Scriptures, and that he appeared to Cephas, and then to the Twelve. After that, he appeared to more than five hundred of the brothers and sisters at the same time, most of whom are still living, though some have fallen asleep. Then he appeared to James, then to all the apostles, and last of all he appeared to me also, as to one abnormally born" (1 Corinthians 15:3-8).

PRAYER

"Lord, I want to live with the reality of the resurrection every day. Your defeat of death and sin empowers me to live a bold, courageous life. Help me do so.

Continue your prayer:

Amen."

Forty

Jesus Is ... OUR SACRIFICE

If you're a baseball fan, you're familiar with the sacrifice bunt and the sacrifice fly. If you've never heard those terms, they are baseball plays in which the batter gives up his opportunity to get a base hit in order to help a runner advance to the next base. It's a selfless play that serves the entire team.

Jesus Christ's sacrifice is the supreme expression of selfless. Author Chuck Swindoll describes it best: "Being unselfish in attitude strikes at the very core of our being. It means we are willing to forgo our own comfort, our own preferences, our own schedule, our own desires for another's benefit. And that brings us back to Christ."[148] Every unselfish act brings us back to Jesus because His death was the ultimate sacrifice.

An email circulated several years ago about a professor of religion, a Dr. Christianson, who gave a simple, but powerful, illustration of what sacrifice looks like. Whether the story is true or not, it brought attention to the fact that those who receive the benefit of Jesus' sacrifice often fail to appreciate its gift.

The professor grew tired of his students' disinterest in the faith, so he came up with a plan. He asked Steve to help, the one student in class with a perfect score. The professor also needed Steve's other asset: he was an incredibly fit athlete, the starting center on the school's football team. Knowing the class had an additional 30 students, the professor asked if Steve could do 300 push-ups in sets of ten. Steve had never done that many, but since he had done 200 push-ups, he accepted the challenge.

The next day in class, the professor carried in an enormous box, featuring the largest, most decorative donuts in town. When the professor explained there was a donut for everyone, the students cheered, sitting up with great anticipation. Dr. Christianson went to Cynthia, the girl in the first row, and asked if she'd like a donut. When she said yes, the professor turned to Steve and asked, "Steve, would you do ten push-ups so that Cynthia can have a donut?" Steve got out from behind his desk and did 10 push-ups.

The class thought that was strange, particularly when the routine continued for the next six students. When Scott, the seventh student, asked if he could do his own push-ups to receive the donut, Dr. Christianson explained that only Steve could do them. "Well, I don't want one, then," Scott answered. Dr. Christianson acknowledged his response, turned to Steve, and asked, "Steve, would you do ten push-ups so Scott can have a donut he doesn't want?" Scott protested, but the professor placed a donut on his desk, instructing Scott to leave it untouched if he didn't want it.

After another dozen students, Steve began to slow down a little and sweat a lot. More students protested, seeking ways to free Steve from their professor's unusual request. When five students remained, Steve grunted and struggled with each push-up. By this time the room was silent, many students shaking their heads in disbelief. When the professor reached Susan, the last girl, and asked if she'd like a donut, she answered with tears streaming down her face. "Dr. Christianson, why can't I help him?" The professor responded with his own tears, explaining that only Steve had a perfect score in class and that he agreed to do this so each student would benefit.

Steve collapsed after doing Susan's 10 push-ups. Dr. Christianson turned to the students and said, "In the same way, Jesus died on the cross, understanding He had done everything required of Him. And like some in this room, many of us leave the gift on the desk, uneaten. My wish is that you might understand and fully comprehend all the riches of grace and mercy that have been given to you through the sacrifice of our Lord and Savior Jesus Christ."

KEY QUOTE

"The whole purpose of the sacrifices in the Old Testament was to shape our thinking so that we would be able to understand why the Son of God had to come into the world. The sacrifices help us to see that in His death on that cross, He did in reality what the sacrifice of animals only did in symbol. Christ made atonement for our sins, and He brings back the presence of God for all who trust in His sacrifice."[149] — Colin Smith

DYK...

The Greek word that Romans 3:25 translates as sacrifice (some translations use 'propitiation') has three meanings:
1) to appease
2) to be merciful
3) to make propitiation for someone

The New Testament never describes people appeasing God. Instead, as Luke 18:13 and 1 John 2:2 make clear, the New Testament describes God as being merciful to, or making propitiation for, us. God provides a merciful expiation, or atonement, of the sins of believers through the death of Christ.[150]

LINK TO YOUR LIFE

Did you know Hebrews 10:17 says that God has memory loss? While memory loss is usually indicative of degenerative disease, God's memory loss concerning our sins is one of his great promises to us. You and I always remember. Even if we're committed to forgiving someone, the memory of the event lingers. Not so with God. When God forgives, he forgets. How is it possible for an all-knowing God to forget anything? "There's no more separation between offender and offendee over the offense. It's gone, completely disappeared. Such forgetting is a gift that few people can give, and none so completely as God. When you pray in faith today for forgiveness, you can forget your sins too. Don't hurt yourself by holding on to guilt over sin that God has wiped from his memory."[151]

SMALL GROUP DISCUSSION

Did the donut illustration connect with you? In what ways? If not, what's another illustration that you like about Jesus' sacrifice? What does Jesus' sacrifice mean to you?

KEY VERSE

"For God presented Jesus as the sacrifice for sin. People are made right with God when they believe that Jesus sacrificed his life, shedding his blood. This sacrifice shows that God was being fair when he held back and did not punish those who sinned in times past, for he was looking ahead and including them in what he would do in this present time. God did this to demonstrate his righteousness, for he himself is fair and just, and he declares sinners to be right in his sight when they believe in Jesus" (Romans 3:25, 26, NLT).

PRAYER

"Jesus, your sacrifice on the cross has changed my eternity. Thank you for all you have done. Help me live in a way that reflects the new life I have been given.

Continue your prayer:

Amen."

Forty-one

Jesus Is ... A DEMONSTRATION OF GOD'S LOVE

According to a survey by the Barna Research Group, 65 percent of adults do not know what John 3:16 means.[152] J. Edwin Hortell creatively brings personality and a fresh look at one of the Bible's most famous verses.

God	the greatest Lover
So loved	the greatest degree
The world	the greatest number
That He gave	the greatest act
His only begotten Son	the greatest gift
That whoever	the greatest invitation
Believes	the greatest simplicity
In Him	the greatest person
Shall not perish	the greatest escape
But	the greatest difference
Have	the greatest certainty
Eternal life	the greatest destiny[153]

Theologian D.A. Carson says it less poetically and more . . . uh . . . directly. "When he says he loves us, does not God . . .

mean something like the following: 'Morally speaking, you are the people of the halitosis, the bulbous nose, the greasy hair, the disjointed knees, the abominable personality. Your sins have made you disgustingly ugly. But I love you anyway, not because you are attractive, but because it is my nature to love.'"[154]

I have three daughters. Each night I make an effort to remind them that I love them and that God loves them. And while my girls are wonderful and beautiful beyond description, I want them to know that neither my love nor God's love is dependent on how they look or act. Certainly my love pales in comparison with how God loves, yet God gives us all a picture of what love is: actively meeting the needs of another without any expectation of payment. And while we could never repay God's demonstration of love, we can offer God's love to others.

KEY QUOTE

"The measure of God's love for us is shown by two things. One is the degree of his sacrifice in saving us from the penalty of our sin. The other is the degree of unworthiness that we had when he saved us."[155] — John Piper

DYK...

There was a British evangelist named Henry Moorehouse whose relationship with Jesus began after years of living what he describes as a "life of vile wickedness." Moorehouse was so moved by God's grace that every time he preached, his Bible text was John 3:16. Each message was different, but his text was always the same.

LINK TO YOUR LIFE

Some people have experienced so much pain and disappointment that they have no interest in eternal life, believing it's an ongoing extension of their current life. Eternal life is different, however. It's "God's life embodied in Christ given to all believers now as a guarantee that they will live forever. Not only will we be changed, almost everything else will also be changed (Revelation 21:1–4). In eternal life there is no death, sickness, enemy, evil, or sin. When we don't know Christ, we make choices as though this life is all we have. In reality, this life is just the introduction to eternity."[156]

Make choices today that are consistent with the hope of a new heaven, a new earth, and a new you.

SMALL GROUP DISCUSSION

Have you ever felt unlovely? Talk about it. Known someone who the world really would not celebrate as beautiful in any way? (Don't use names or identities.) Talk about them. Talk about the reality that God loves each person the same, and with the same intensity.

KEY VERSE

"But God showed his great love for us by sending Christ to die for us while we were still sinners" (Romans 5:8, NLT).

PRAYER

"God, your grace is unexplainable, but it is visual in Jesus. Thank you for demonstrating your love for me and for all of humanity.

Continue your prayer:

Amen."

Forty-two
Jesus Is ... COMMITTED TO US

I'd like to think I'd be committed to those I love, regardless of circumstances. But I'd have a hard time committing to strangers, or those I didn't love. Thankfully for all of us, Jesus is not like me. The apostle Paul reminds us that Jesus "loved us and gave himself up for us" (Ephesians 5:2). He was and is committed to us, no matter what.

Dave Roever is a Vietnam vet who served as a forward gunner with the U.S. Navy's elite Brown Water, Black Beret. He was severely wounded when a white phosphorus grenade exploded six inches from his face, leaving his body burned beyond recognition. Medics were able to stabilize his condition until he could be transferred and treated in a burn ward back in the states. He looked forward to seeing Brenda, his new bride, but he was anxious for how she'd respond to his physical condition.

His worst fears materialized when a woman walked into the room.

Dave identified her as the wife of another injured man in his room, recognizing her from the picture displayed beside his bed. It was clear she was uncomfortable. She contorted her face and covered her nose from the smell of burnt flesh. Because the dozen patients in the room were so disfigured, the woman could not recognize her husband. Dave watched her go from bed to bed, reading the name on the clipboard that hung from the foot of each bed. Finally she found her husband. After double-checking the name, she slowly walked up to him.

Dave had rehearsed what this scene might look like upon Brenda's arrival a million times in his mind, but of all the potential scenarios, Dave had not considered this one. The woman took off her wedding ring and placed it on the night stand beside her picture. As she turned to walk away, a nurse stopped her, asking her to wait before making such a drastic decision. Dave watched her push the nurse aside and say, "I couldn't be seen with him." She forever walked out of his life.

Dave was grateful his friend was asleep, but his own nightmare had just begun. Although he hoped Brenda would not respond the same way, he prepared himself for the worst. Brenda arrived the next afternoon, and Dave noticed the initial horror on her face everyone first exhibits, despite attempts to veil the shock. She, too, began going bed to bed, reading names to find him. Dave closed his eyes, not wanting to face the potential reality. He heard her approaching with slow, measured steps. Brenda wore the perfume Dave purchased for her before he left. Not able to wait any longer, he opened his eyes just as she kissed him on the worst part of his burned face and whispered in his ear, "Welcome home, Davey. Welcome home."[157]

Jesus cares about your past, present, and future, and nothing will alter his commitment, regardless of your condition. Instead, be confident Jesus will whisper and shout to show that his commitment is eternal.

Welcome home.

KEY QUOTE

"It is this absolute confidence in Jesus' commitment to us that gives us the strength to live and die with Him, and to endure whatever comes."[158] — Larry Richards

DYK...

It's important to evaluate to whom or what we commit, as evidenced by two marriages in recent years. In 2011, a woman married herself. (Yes, you read that correctly.) In 2007 another woman married the Eiffel Tower, changing her last name to Eiffel. Brian McLaren writes that "[Passion] can easily degenerate into sentimental or cheesy or hotheaded or hardheaded or softheaded, and too often it has done so."[159] Jesus' commitment isn't sentimental or cheesy. He loves us, warts and all, and invites us to commit to follow Him.

LINK TO YOUR LIFE

Because of Jesus' commitment, these are a few things we no longer have to worry about:
- solving every problem
- controlling every situation
- living with regret
- wondering if your relationship with God is secure
- giving up
- being overwhelmed by fear
- being good enough

In place of those worries, we are now free to trust, love, encourage, serve, give thanks, and dare to courageously follow God.

SMALL GROUP DISCUSSION

Talk about commitment: Where is it common in the world; where is it not? How's your commitment to God these days? In what ways is it strong? In what ways would you like to see it improve?

KEY VERSE

"May you experience the love of Christ, though it is too great to understand fully" (Ephesians 3:19, NLT).

PRAYER

"Jesus, thank you for being one thing I can rely on in life. Your love never fails.

Continue your prayer:

Amen."

Forty-three
Jesus Is ... A RANSOM FOR MANY

Frank Sinatra Jr., Eric Peugeot, Kyoko Chan Cox (daughter of Yoko Ono), and Charles Lindbergh Jr., all have one thing in common. They were children of celebrities who were kidnapped and held for ransom. The ransom price for kidnappings have varied through the years, with the Guinness Book of Records reporting $60 million as the largest amount ever paid to redeem someone.

The Bible describes Jesus as our ransom. Instead of dollars being exchanged, however, Jesus gave his life for our lives. Many have asked who received this ransom, and author John Piper says the biblical response would surely be God. "The Bible says that Christ 'gave Himself up for us, [an] . . . offering . . . to God' (Ephesians 5:2). Christ 'offered himself without blemish to God' (Hebrews 9:14)."[160] In the book of Romans, the apostle Paul says that because of the price Christ paid, we are no longer under any condemnation of God. We are free! More than that, we are healed, restored, and forgiven. D.M. Lloyd Jones sums it up well: "Everything is in Christ. There is nothing further that we can desire. He will satisfy your every need, whatever your need may be. He is with you in every respect and in every circumstance."[161]

Hebrews 12:2 tells us to fix our eyes on Jesus. But from time to time it's also good to look at ourselves, remembering what Jesus has done in our lives and where we'd be apart from him. Reflecting on what God has done on my behalf is humbling, and it helps me connect with God on a deeper level. The price has been paid. I am now free in Jesus. Free to love, free to serve, and free to celebrate my forgiveness.

KEY QUOTE

"In times of war, many sons have given their lives for what they believe in. We call them heroes. Yeshua, God's only son, is the greatest hero. He willingly gave his life as a ransom—not just for a country but for the whole world."[162] — Elizabeth L. Vander Meulen

DYK . . .

Often in movies, criminals create ransom notes using clippings from newspapers so forensic experts aren't able to identify their handwriting. There is a fun online ransom note creator you can find at http://ransom.sytes.org/. (Listing this site is for fun only and does not support writing actual ransom notes, if there were any doubt!)

LINK TO YOUR LIFE

We don't take enough time to realize the value of our lives. We are not insignificant. Jesus' death on the cross is personalized when we identify that his life was given up on our behalf. We were rescued to live without guilt and with purpose.

SMALL GROUP DISCUSSION

There are lots of movies and books about being kidnapped. Discuss any favorites. Describe what you think it would be like to be kidnapped and held for ransom. What would it feel like to be ransomed and freed?

KEY VERSE

"For even the Son of Man did not come to be served, but to serve, and to give his life as a ransom for many" (Mark 10:45, NLT).

PRAYER

"Heavenly Father, no one but Jesus could bring me to you. Thank you for offering Jesus and receiving his payment so that I may live.

Continue your prayer:

Amen."

Forty-four
Jesus Is ... LIFE-CHANGING

The life of Jesus split time. Our calendar is measured according to his birth. Even scholars who prefer to use B.C.E./C.E. (Before the Common Era/The Common Era) instead of B.C./A.D. (Before Christ/Anno Domini or year of our Lord), do so with the understanding that the "common era" begins with the life of Christ. Jesus changes everything.

A sermon excerpt attributed to James Allen Francis describes Jesus' humble beginnings that eventually changed eternity:

> He was born in an obscure village, the child of a peasant. He grew up in another village, where he worked in a carpenter shop until he was 30. Then, for three years, he was an itinerant preacher.
>
> He never wrote a book. He never held an office. He never had a family or owned a home. He didn't go to college. He never lived in a big city. He never traveled 200 miles from the place where he was born. He did none of the things that usually accompany greatness. He had no credentials but himself.
>
> He was only 33 when the tide of public opinion

turned against him. His friends ran away. One of them denied him. He was turned over to his enemies and went through the mockery of a trial. He was nailed to a cross between two thieves. While he was dying, his executioners gambled for his garments, the only property he had on earth. When he was dead, he was laid in a borrowed grave, through the pity of a friend.

[Twenty] centuries have come and gone, and today he is the central figure of the human race. I am well within the mark when I say that all the armies that ever marched, all the navies that ever sailed, all the parliaments that ever sat, all the kings that ever reigned — put together — have not affected the life of man on this earth as much as that one, solitary life.[163]

"Writing in *Time* magazine, novelist Reynolds Price remarked, 'It would require much exotic calculation, however, to deny that the single most powerful figure—not merely in these two millenniums but in all human history — has been Jesus of Nazareth.' When we consider the bare details of His life — a brief life of approximately 34 years — the impact He had is astonishing."[164]

KEY QUOTE

"Just think: Every promise God has ever made finds its fulfillment in Jesus. God doesn't just give us grace; he gives us Jesus, the Lord of grace. If it's peace, it's only found in Jesus, the Prince of Peace. Even life itself is found in the Resurrection and the Life. Christianity isn't all that complicated . . . it's Jesus."[165] — Joni Eareckson Tada

DYK...

... that no matter who you are or where you're from or what you've done, Jesus wants to change your life?

... that a day doesn't go by without Jesus calling you, loving you, and ready to lead you?

... there isn't anything too big Jesus can't handle nor anything too small he doesn't care about?

... that my best days remind me Jesus is with me, and my worst days remind me he hasn't forgotten me?

... that Jesus is with you right now?

LINK TO YOUR LIFE

Have you allowed Jesus to change your life? What is one area in which you have seen change? What is one area for which you continue to pray?

SMALL GROUP DISCUSSION

Talk about change. Why is it difficult? Why do people resist it? Is there good change? What type of change does Jesus offer?

KEY VERSE

"Come to me, all you who are weary and burdened, and I will give you rest" (Matthew 11:28).

PRAYER

"Jesus, there is none like you. None. Help me remember that today and to remain faithful to you.

Continue your prayer:

Amen."

Forty-five
Jesus Is ... APPROACHABLE

Ever feel embarrassed?
Disconnected?
Ashamed?
> Jesus welcomes you.

Ever have a bad reputation?
Say the wrong thing?
Wish you were dead?
> Jesus welcomes you.

Ever scorned?
Disrespected?
Ignored?
> Jesus welcomes you.

You might feel rejected, but you're not.
You might wander aimlessly, but you're not lost.
You might despise what you did, but your life's not over.

Approach Jesus with confidence. He's waiting.

KEY QUOTE

"Alexander, Caesar, Charlemagne and myself founded empires. But on what did we rest the creations of our genius? Upon sheer force. Jesus Christ alone founded His empire upon love; and at this hour millions of men will die for Him."[166] — Napoleon Bonaparte

DYK ...

Matthew threw a party for his tax collecting friends and others with notorious reputations so they could meet Jesus. Even though the religious leaders despised him and his friends, Matthew knew Jesus would welcome them. Matthew gave up great financial wealth to be with Jesus and gain acceptance, spiritual wealth, and a life mission.

LINK TO YOUR LIFE

Is anything keeping you from Jesus? Many would confidently tell others Jesus is approachable while privately fearful Jesus might reject them. Take time to thank Jesus for always being available, or ask Jesus to forgive any doubt that he would.

SMALL GROUP DISCUSSION

On a scale of 1-10 (10 = highly approachable), how approachable do you feel Jesus is? Have there been times in your life when you would've answered differently? What makes the difference?

KEY VERSE

"Later, Matthew invited Jesus and his disciples to his home as dinner guests, along with many tax collectors and other disreputable sinners. But when the Pharisees saw this, they asked his disciples, 'Why does your teacher eat with such scum?'" (Matthew 9:10, 11, NLT)

PRAYER

"Jesus, thank you for being approachable at all times and in all circumstances.

Continue your prayer:

Amen."

SECTION 4: The Holy Spirit is . . .

Forty-six
The Holy Spirit . . . IS GOD

Jeremy Lin, the New York Knicks' point guard for the 2011-2012 season, graduated from Harvard University. Impressive. He also started for Harvard's basketball team. Not as impressive. At least, that was the opinion on NBA draft day, when Lin was not selected, effectively ending his dream to play professional basketball. But in true underdog fashion, he refused to give up, worked hard, and managed to get signed by an NBA team.

He rarely played and spent most of his first year watching from the bench, but in his second year on his third team, Jeremy got his break. Two months into the season as a member of the Knicks, Lin got the opportunity to play because of injuries to other players. Lin was impressive. He led the Knicks to seven straight victories, stole headlines from the New York tabloids, and won the hearts of basketball fans and underdog lovers worldwide. "Linsanity" was born.

"What made the difference?" reporters and radio and TV personalities asked. Everyone wondered how an unknown could go from obscurity to glory so quickly. Clearly, Lin had talent. Why hadn't anyone previously noticed?

The same could be said of the Holy Spirit, the third member

of the Trinity. Admittedly, this illustration is quite a stretch and Jeremy Lin, a strong believer in Jesus, would shudder at being compared to the Holy Spirit. But there is one interesting parallel. Few, it appears, give the Holy Spirit much credit, yet the Spirit is part of the Trinity, resulting in divine status. I can imagine the reporters asking, "What? The Holy Spirit is God?"

Let's consider the Spirit's stats:

He knows all things (1 Corinthians 2:11)

He is everywhere present (Psalm 139:7-10)

He is all-powerful (Romans 15:19)

He is eternal (Hebrews 9:14)

All qualities indicate deity. And just to make it exceedingly clear, in Acts 5:1-4, the Holy Spirit is even called God. It is, in fact, a stunning resume. In the *New Christian's Handbook*, Max Anders writes, "The Holy Spirit is not religious fervor or a righteous attitude. He is God. He usually stays in the background of our spiritual life, holding things together. But He is no less necessary than gravity to the earth. Without both, everything would go flying apart."

Jeremy Lin had his blazing media moment in the sun, but I bet the Holy Spirit could take him one-on-one. He's probably got awesome hang time.

KEY QUOTE

"If you don't believe what the Bible teaches about the Holy Spirit . . .

- You may get a twisted notion of who the Holy Spirit is, believing that He is not a real person and not God.
- You may get confused about the trustworthiness of the Bible, because the Bible treats Him as a person and as God.
- You may lose the ability to trust in Him for your daily life because you don't realize He is there to help you.
- You may lose the peace that comes from believing that He is

there, He can help, and He wants to help."[167] — Max Anders

DYK . . .

Millard Erickson writes, "The Holy Spirit, being fully divine, is to be accorded the same honor and respect that we give to the Father and the Son. It is appropriate to worship him as we do them. He should not be thought of as in any sense inferior in essence to them, although his role may sometimes be subordinated to theirs."[168]

LINK TO YOUR LIFE

The Holy Spirit speaks to us and guides us. How are you doing as a listener? Can you hear him speak? Are you obeying him?

SMALL GROUP DISCUSSION

Share about what you have traditionally thought about the Holy Spirit. How is your thinking changing? How can he be a greater part of your life?

KEY VERSE

"*Teach me to do your will, for you are my God; may your good Spirit lead me on level ground*" (Psalm 143:10).

PRAYER

"Holy Spirit, thank you for living inside me. I want to follow and obey you in every way. Help me do that today.

Continue your prayer:

Amen."

Forty-seven
The Holy Spirit...
EMPOWERS US

The human body is rather remarkable. Despite all of its intricate design and capabilities, maintenance is rather minimal. Granted, for optimum performance, proper care is required. But plenty of people survive with little to no physical or mental upkeep, as evidenced by humor websites like failblog.org.

It's not the same with our spiritual lives, at least not the way God intended. Romans 8:11 says, "The Spirit of God, who raised Jesus from the dead, lives in you. And just as God raised Christ Jesus from the dead, he will give life to your mortal bodies by this same Spirit living within you" (NLT). The Holy Spirit gives life and empowers us to live for God. In fact, according to that verse, the same Spirit that raised Jesus from the dead is available to me, too. Wow! I don't often live with that kind of understanding. What would my life look like if it were fully empowered by God?

The following reveals how God's Spirit is ready to empower us:

- power to witness — to show and tell the love of Jesus (Acts 1:8)
- power to serve (1 Corinthians 12:1)
- power to pray (Romans 8:26)
- power to overcome spiritual opposition (Matthew 12:28)

That list makes me realize I often ignore what God wants to do in my life because it's challenging or intimidating. It's easier to pursue "safer" Christian activities. But safer for whom or what? My reputation? I don't want to miss out on the Holy Spirit's power. After Jesus fasted and was tempted in the desert, Luke wrote that Jesus returned to Galilee in the power of the Holy Spirit. Despite incredible physical and spiritual fatigue, God's Spirit empowered Jesus to minister. It would have been reasonable for Jesus to take a two-week vacation, or at least a comp day or two. Instead, he ministered, strengthened by the Holy Spirit.

There was a story in a Kentucky paper years ago about a local man who struggled to start his car. Upon further inspection, he discovered someone had stolen his motor! The good news is that for believers, God's Spirit isn't going anywhere. The Holy Spirit is ready to give our lives engine-like power. You and I just need to turn the keys to our spiritual lives and be willing to follow as God leads.

KEY QUOTE

"The early church was birthed into an environment of sorcerers, gods, goddesses, and many spiritual cults and religions. We are not facing anything new. We are not facing anything that the Holy Spirit of God . . . cannot overcome."[169] — Dan Kimball

DYK . . .

Romans 6:6-8 and 1 Corinthians 3:1-4 reveal two ways to live the Christian life. One is to be powered by our own thoughts and desires, the other by God's Spirit. While God has won the battle for the souls of those who will commit to him, the battle for the minds and bodies of men and women — even Christians — continues. Depending on when we have given our lives to Jesus, we have all those preceding years of habits focused on satisfying our own wants and desires. The Holy Spirit is working at changing those so they're now consistent with God's will for our lives . . . but it is a battle. The good news is that just as God has won many hearts for eternity, he can win the moment-by-moment battles.

God's Spirit will give us all the power we need, but we need to follow him.

LINK TO YOUR LIFE

In his commentary on Romans, Bruce Barton offers excellent tips on allowing the Holy Spirit to empower our lives:

- Ask for greater openness and responsiveness to the Holy Spirit's guidance.
- Consciously humble ourselves before God, so we are not too proud to change.
- Look to God's Word for guidance.
- Obey where we have clear direction, so that our forward movement will enhance the Holy Spirit's leading. (It makes little sense to steer a parked car!)

When was the last time you prayed as Jesus did, "Nevertheless, may your will, not mine, be done"?[170]

SMALL GROUP DISCUSSION

What are some things or areas in your life that just seem . . . impossible to change? What if, with God and his Spirit, you could begin to change them?

KEY VERSE

"But you will receive power when the Holy Spirit comes upon you. And you will be my witnesses, telling people about me everywhere — in Jerusalem, throughout Judea, in Samaria, and to the ends of the earth" (Acts 1:8, NLT).

PRAYER

"Holy Spirit, Thank you for the choices you provide, the invitation to follow you moment by moment. Help me choose you today, all day.

Continue your prayer:

Amen."

Forty-eight
The Holy Spirit...
LIVES WITHIN US

I've got space issues. Whether holding my breath in an effort to make myself smaller in a crowded elevator, or backing away from a close talker, I need space. I can pinpoint the moment I first recognized I had proximity problems: my MRI. That tube of terror, a seemingly mild piece of machinery, gave me fits during my 30 minutes inside and more than 20 years since. Thankfully, technological advances now provide open MRIs, but that one experience taught me a lot about prayer.

For a guy who loves open space, I'm actually grateful the Holy Spirit is not far off. The Spirit is so close, in fact, as to actually enter into each believer. That's incredibly close. The moment you became a believer, a sign went up in the window of your soul boasting, "Occupied." So what benefit is there to God's Spirit living inside of us? One is the opportunity to have God lead and direct our lives. Ephesians 5 says we are to be filled with God's Spirit, which means to be controlled by his Spirit. In other words, we are to obey God and live under his influence rather than our own. Bruce Barton writes, "Just as a drunk is influenced by alcohol, so a believer should be controlled by the Spirit. However, there are important differences. The drunk loses self-control, but the Spirit gives the believer self-control. The drunk has an artificial happiness that does not last, while the Spirit-filled believer has a deep joy in the Lord. Drunken people do stupid things that hurt others and bring them embarrassment, but Spirit-filled believers help others and live to the glory of God."[171]

It's actually an amazing opportunity. Sadly, we often give up the fulfillment of a satisfying spiritual life for temporary satisfaction. That's my excuse, at least.

Fortunately, this is yet another example of the goodness of God. His Holy Spirit always remains within. Author Chuck Swindoll writes that the New Testament doesn't give any indication that the Holy Spirit would ever leave a believer. He points out that when the apostles challenged believers to live godly lives, it was for the purpose of bringing glory to God. There was no indication that they might lose the Spirit if they failed to do so. "The permanent presence of the Holy Spirit in the lives of all believers is guaranteed by the Father's response to Christ's prayer: 'And I will ask the Father, and he will give you another advocate to help you and be with you forever' (John 14:16). There are no conditions or exceptions to this promise."[172]

KEY QUOTE

"Deity indwelling men! That, I say, is Christianity, and no man has experienced rightly the power of Christian belief until he has known this for himself as a living reality. Everything else is preliminary to this."[173] — A.W.Tozer

DYK . . .

Professor and poet Calvin Miller writes, "God . . . does not lavish his children with a jolly discipleship so that they may swim in spiritual ecstasy between conversion and death. God is a giver, but he does not give happiness. He gives redemption, meaning, security, love, victory, and the indwelling of the Holy Spirit. And happiness is our response to his gifts."[174]

LINK TO YOUR LIFE

Ever feel that inner nudge to say or do something? Say hello to the Holy Spirit. Living a Spirit-filled life means we obey God's promptings. Some argue those aren't always from God. But if they provide an opportunity to do or say something that will encourage people or introduce them to Jesus, that's a good indication it's from God.

Commit to following through when God's Spirit prompts you this week.

SMALL GROUP DISCUSSION

Talk about the implications of having a living Spirit, an eternal force for good, living inside of you. Share how you think he has worked in your life. Share ways that, quite possibly, you have kept him from working.

KEY VERSE

"After they prayed, the place where they were meeting was shaken. And they were all filled with the Holy Spirit and spoke the word of God boldly" (Acts 4:31).

PRAYER

"Holy Spirit, thank you for being a permanent resident in my life. If it were up to me, I would have left my disobedient self a long time ago. Thank you for staying and helping me learn obedience.

Continue your prayer:

Amen."

Forty-nine
The Holy Spirit ... PURIFIES US

Purifying silver is time-consuming . . . and dangerous. It requires many rounds of filtering impure materials as the silver is heated at extraordinary temperatures. Each time, impurities are removed until finally, the silversmith has attained such purity he can see his reflection in the silver.

The Holy Spirit does the same in our lives, except the Spirit wants to see the reflection of Christ in our lives.

The Holy Spirit is aptly named, considering one of his primary activities is to purify and cleanse us, or make us holy. In 1 Corinthians 6 and Titus 3, the apostle Paul describes this as God's washing and renewal process. That actually sounds pleasant, as if our purifications were as simple as washing clothes. Set the cycle, water level, and temperature, add detergent, and press start. Thirty to 40 minutes later, the machine produces clean clothes. Unfortunately, it's not as easy with our lives. Many times, the Holy Spirit washes and rewashes us. Sometimes he lets us soak to facilitate the renewal process; other times he hand-washes us to scrub out stubborn stains.

If you've ever been frustrated that you're not growing at the rate you'd like or continue to stumble in the same ways, you're not alone. Paul distressingly cried out, "I don't really understand myself, for I want to do what is right, but I don't do it. Instead, I do what I hate" (Romans 7:15, NLT). Thankfully, the Holy Spirit doesn't toss us aside as we might a piece of clothing we're unable to clean. Instead, he continues to mold and shape us until we are formed in the image of Christ. The challenge is sometimes that the molding and shaping is done against our will. If you feel the heat being turned up in your life, recognize God is at work. Is God prompting you to start doing something or stop doing something? Listen and obey.

It beats another round in the spin cycle.

KEY QUOTE

"The Holy Spirit is pure, for He is the Holy Spirit. He is wise, for He is the Spirit of wisdom. He is true, for He is the Spirit of truth. He is like Jesus, for He is the Spirit of Christ. He is like the Father, for He is the Spirit of the Father. He wants to be the Lord of your life, and He wants to possess you so that you are no longer in command of the little vessel in which you sail. You may be a passenger on board, or one of the crew, but you definitely are not in charge. Someone else is in command of the vessel."[175] — A.W. Tozer

DYK...

As the Holy Spirit purifies us, he's transforming us, metamorphosing us into Christlikeness. The Greek verb *metamorphomai* means transform and is where we get our English word, metamorphosis. Romans 12:2 uses the verb form, saying we are to be transformed. 2 Corinthians 3:18 also uses the verb, saying we are being transformed (metamorphosed) into Christ's image.

LINK TO YOUR LIFE

Ask God to purify your life. Don't be surprised when that prayer is answered. The process is not always pleasant, but the outcome is worth it.

SMALL GROUP DISCUSSION

What would it mean to be absolutely purified from every last wrongful thing you've done? Can such a promise be believed? How? Can a Christian believe this?

KEY VERSE

"So I say, let the Holy Spirit guide your lives. Then you won't be doing what your sinful nature craves" (Galatians 5:16, NLT).

PRAYER

"'Search me, God, and know my heart. Test me and know my anxious thoughts. See if there is any offensive way in me, and lead me in the way everlasting.' [Taken from David in Psalm 139:23, 24.]

Continue your prayer:

Amen."

Fifty

The Holy Spirit . . .
GIVES GIFTS TO US

There are no atheists in foxholes or in classrooms during final exams. Fortunately, God is real, and he gives gifts to all who believe. However, Nicky Gumbel clarifies, "I do not believe God will answer the prayer of the student who turned in his test and prayed, 'O God, please let Paris be the capital of England!'"[176] God is gracious, but he doesn't rearrange geography.

But God does give gifts. The Holy Spirit gives each believer at least one spiritual gift, a special ability for the purpose of strengthening the church. Many times it is consistent with a person's natural gifting, but not always. I have a friend who is the cheapest man on the planet (*his* words, not mine). He will not spend money on anything. But he has the spiritual gift of giving. He frequently and generously provides money to individuals and organizations who serve God.

Spiritual gifts are addressed in five key Bible passages that cover four books: 1 Corinthians, Romans, Ephesians, and 1 Peter. Because I like food, I always remember those books. (They spell crepé; I added the é.) Paul addresses the topic in three of his books, and Peter in one of his. Some key thoughts on the subject:

- There are many gifts, but all are given by the Holy Spirit.

- Through the gifts, we form one body, allowing us to function interdependently.
- There is a difference between "gifts of the Spirit" and "fruit of the Spirit." Gifts identify what we do, and fruit reveals our character.
- There is a difference between natural abilities, acquired abilities, and spiritual abilities.
- Many spiritual gifts are also commands. For example, some people have the gift of giving and serving and evangelism, but all believers are commanded to give, serve, and share their faith.
- We are to practice, study, and develop our gifts.

Everyone likes gifts, especially receiving them. But spiritual gifts are ones we *give away* to serve others. I watched my daughter use her gifts of encouragement and artistry today as she made her grandmother several gifts. Her grandmother's response was all my daughter needed to know that there is value in using your gifts to serve others. Evaluate what gifts the Holy Spirit has given you, and pray for clarity as needed. That prayer is more likely to be answered than the student who hoped Paris was England's capital. I'm not sure what spiritual gift that student had, but let's hope his teacher's was mercy.

KEY QUOTE

"Because our gifts carry us out into the world and make us participants in life, the uncovering of them is one of the most important tasks confronting any one of us."[177] — Elizabeth O'Connor

DYK . . .

The Bible does not provide a definitive list of spiritual gifts. Twenty are mentioned by name, and they tend to fall into three general categories.

- Leadership gifts serve the church in public roles, such as pastor-teacher or evangelist.
- Service gifts provide strength and support for the overall function of the church, in areas like hospitality, encouragement, serving, giving, and faith.
- Miraculous gifts are used by God to demonstrate his power to others.

LINK TO YOUR LIFE

Have you identified your spiritual gift(s)? Ask your pastor if your church offers a spiritual gift test. Ask friends from your church what gift they think you might have. What areas of ministry are you passionate about? Which bring you joy?

SMALL GROUP DISCUSSION

What are the greatest gifts you've ever been given by another person? What do you believe are the greatest gifts given by God? Given to you personally by God? How do the gifts from others and the gifts from God compare?

KEY VERSE

"*God has given each of you a gift from his great variety of spiritual gifts. Use them well to serve one another*" (1 Peter 4:10, NLT).

PRAYER

"God, help me to identify and use my gifts to serve and honor you.

Continue your prayer:

Amen."

Fifty-one
The Holy Spirit . . . SECURES US

If you're under 20, you don't know a world without Ziploc bags. Twenty years ago TV commercials (and yes, we had color then) wowed us with the latest sandwich bag technology. It was now possible to seal in flavor and freshness. Trust me, that was a big deal. I tested the theory with a teaching illustration while speaking at a youth retreat. While attempting to illustrate that the Holy Spirit secures our relationship with Christ, I placed my large set of keys in a Ziploc bag, applied the safety seal, and violently shook the bag upside down, attempting to break the seal and free the keys. Not a chance. That seal was solid and held my keys securely.

2 Corinthians 1:22 says that Christ "set his seal of ownership on us, and put his Spirit in our hearts as a deposit, guaranteeing what is to come." The Holy Spirit's seal implies security, authenticity, and ownership. The Spirit is God's guarantee that our salvation is secure. His seal can never be broken.

"Registered mail furnishes a good example of the security concept in sealing. When registering a piece of mail, it not only has to be sealed carefully, but then the post office stamps it a number of times across the edges of the seal to be able to detect any tampering with that seal. Only two people can legitimately break the seal, the recipient or the sender (if it is delivered back to him). In the case of believers, God is the Sender, and God is the Recipient, and God is the One who does the sealing."[178]

The Holy Spirit is God's pledge that he will not go back on any of his promises. Regardless of the status of your relationships, job, or financial position, you can rest in the fact that God offers a secure relationship, one that is sealed by the Holy Spirit.

KEY QUOTE

"Life is uncertain and we should say, 'If the Lord permits.' Yet we can live securely because we have the promises of God in our hands and the Spirit of God in our hearts.[179] — Robert Morgan

DYK . . .

In ancient times, people used seals to confirm a document's authenticity (see Jeremiah 32:10). Archaeologists have discovered more than 1,200 seals from the Old Testament period.[180]

LINK TO YOUR LIFE

Do you struggle to believe God is *for* you? Sometimes we just need an image or symbol to remind us of what's true. Throughout your day, take time to find as many illustrations as possible that reveal your relationship with God is secure. Here are some to get you started:

- When you zip up your jacket, let it remind you that God protects you
- When you put food in plastic containers, think about how God seals you
- When you tie a shoe, thank God for securing you

SMALL GROUP DISCUSSION

What things in life give you security? What do many people seek for their security? How is God's gift of security different?

KEY VERSE

"It's in Christ that you, once you heard the truth and believed it (this Message of your salvation), found yourselves home free — signed, sealed, and delivered by the Holy Spirit" (Ephesians 1:13, The Message).

PRAYER

"Dear God, your Holy Spirit is such a gift. You have provided all I need. Help me live with the knowledge that my relationship with you is secure. Help me focus on the truth from the Bible rather than lies from the devil.

Continue your prayer:

Amen."

Fifty-two
The Holy Spirit ... PRAYS FOR US

I was in over my head. It was my first year as a public school teacher and I had no experience, no curriculum, no mentor, and not a clue what to do. I did have youthful hope, however, so I took a six-foot piece of paper off the roll in the limited teacher's supply closet and wrote "WANTED" in large block letters across the top of the page. Then I wrote each of the following words under one another, with a check box beside each: Love, Joy, Peace, Patience, Kindness, Goodness, Faithfulness, Gentleness, Self Control. I wasn't allowed to put Bible verses on the wall — overtly, at least — but I was able to list the fruit of the Spirit from Galatians 5:22, 23 in this subtle way. It was a way to remind me to focus on God's Spirit throughout the day while hopefully casting some vision for students whose eyes wandered during my lesson.

There were so many times during my first year of teaching that I felt completely overwhelmed and ill-equipped. Many times, out of desperation, I would look at that sign on my wall as a way of begging God for help. I didn't know what to pray other than, "Ahhhhhh!" Fortunately, God's Spirit took over and, according to Romans 8:26, 27, prayed on my behalf.

The Holy Spirit knows us far better than we know ourselves. He knows exactly what we need, when we need it, and how to pray for it. Are you in a difficult place, or completely perplexed on what next step to take? Turn to God and share your heart. And when you don't know what to pray, tell God you are at a loss for words and need his help. And then be still. Allow the Holy Spirit to pray on your behalf.

My "WANTED" sign started a few conversations with students during the year, but it served as a constant reminder of what I wanted: more of God's peace and leadership in my life. I did feel God's power and presence in my life, and I pray that you do too. Take time right now to focus on God and to rest in his presence.

KEY QUOTE

"The spiritual quality of a prayer is determined not by its intensity but by its origin. In evaluating prayer, we should inquire who is doing the praying — our determined hearts or the Holy Spirit? If the prayer originates with the Holy Spirit, then the wrestling can be beautiful and wonderful; but if we are the victims of our own overheated desires, our praying can be as carnal as any other act."[181] — A.W. Tozer

DYK . . .

Max Lucado reminds us that the Holy Spirit is "the presence of God in our lives, carrying on the work of Jesus. The Holy Spirit helps us in three directions — inwardly (by granting us the fruits of the Spirit, Galatians 5:22–24), upwardly (by praying for us, Romans 8:26) and outwardly (by pouring God's love into our hearts, Romans 5:5)."[182]

LINK TO YOUR LIFE

Instead of praying for something or someone, be still. Listen. What is God saying? Take time to thank God for what he is doing in your life. Thank God that he is with you. Conclude with more stillness.

SMALL GROUP DISCUSSION

Share why you have confidence or doubt that the Holy Spirit prays for you. Would it make a difference in your life if the Spirit did? How?

KEY VERSE

"Meanwhile, the moment we get tired in the waiting, God's Spirit is right alongside helping us along. If we don't know how or what to pray, it doesn't matter. He does our praying in and for us, making prayer out of our wordless sighs, our aching groans. He knows us far better than we know ourselves, knows our pregnant condition, and keeps us present before God" (Romans 8:26, 27, The Message).

PRAYER

"Holy Spirit, I give my day to you. You know what I need and how to pray. Lift me up to the Father, that He may be glorified through me.

Continue your prayer:

Amen."

Curriculum Ideas

How to use *52 Reasons to Believe* in a group or class

OPTION 1: SURVEY STUDY (4-8 WEEKS)
4-8 week survey of entire book
Select 1-2 chapters from each topic:
Bible, God, Jesus Christ, Holy Spirit
–OR–
4-8 week study on ONE topic:
Bible, God, Jesus Christ, Holy Spirit

OPTION 2 : QUARTERLY STUDY (12 WEEKS)
12 week study of entire book
- Select three chapters from Bible
- Select three chapters from God
- Select three chapters from Jesus
- Select three chapters from Holy Spirit

–OR–

12 week study on one topic
- 12 weeks on God
- 12 weeks on Bible
- 12 weeks on Jesus
- 12 weeks on Jesus & the Holy Spirit (6-8 chapters from Jesus and 4-6 from Holy Spirit)

OPTION 3 : YEAR-LONG STUDY (52 WEEKS)
Study one chapter each week

Lesson Template

EACH LESSON HAS 5 KEY ELEMENTS

5 minutes: Welcome
5 minutes: Opener
10 minutes: Study
20 minutes: Discuss
10 minutes: Apply

Ideas for each section

WELCOME

Goal: Help people get settled and connect to one another
- Allow people to mix/mingle.
- Invite a few group members share a highlight or challenge from their week.
- Share announcements pertinent to the group.
- Play a get-to-know-you game like 'Would You Rather.' (Use any discussion starter or talk trigger type of resource.)

OPENER

Goal: Help people connect to the topic
- Beforehand, survey the lesson and come up with a provocative question to get people talking. (For example, from chapter 1: "Is it possible that Jesus doubted the Bible's validity?" or "How can we know how Jesus felt about the Bible?")
- Ask a True/False question, based on the topic, to get people talking (For example, from chapter 1: "True or False? It is wrong to have doubts about the Bible." or "True or False? It is healthy to have doubts about the Bible.)
- Use the KEY QUOTE as a catalyst for discussion. (For example, from chapter 1: "Robert Harris says, '_____.' Do you agree or disagree? Why?")

STUDY

Goal: Get people into the study and the Bible
- Read the main chapter content and ask for feedback
- Follow up the main content by having everyone read and look up the KEY VERSE. Ask how the verse connects to the content.
- Add the DID YOU KNOW (DYK) portion of the chapter. Ask for feedback and whether others have additional insight to the topic.

DISCUSS

Goal: Help people discuss the topic and how it relates to their lives
- Depending on the size of your group/class, you can do this as one group or gather into smaller groups. If you have ten or more people, it is recommended to get into multiple groups.
- Use the SMALL GROUP DISCUSSION and LINK TO YOUR LIFE sections to facilitate conversation.

APPLY

Goal: Help people connect to the topic
- Stay in small groups or re-gather as one large group.
- Share highlights from the lesson.
- Share a goal or commitment made that will help each person apply the material to their lives. (The LINK TO YOUR LIFE section helps with this.)
- Pray for one another.

Use *52 Reasons to Believe* and *52 Ways to Grow* together
Each person will walk away with an application point from
your *Reasons to Believe* study. But, add an opportunity for
group members to incorporate a spiritual growth idea during
the week between their group or class.

Lessons would retain the 5 key elements, but during the last
element (APPLY), group members report how their spiritual
growth idea went. Then as a wrap-up, have everyone identify
which spiritual growth idea they'll try the following week.

WAYS TO SELECT IDEAS:

- Group leader selects one
- Group leader selects 2-3, and members select one of those
- Each week, a different person from the group, selects 1 or
  more ideas for group to try.
- Each person selects their own idea. (OK for more than one
  person to select the same idea.)

Endnotes

1 Tan, P. L. (1996). *Encyclopedia of 7700 Illustrations: Signs of the Times*. Garland, TX: Bible Communications, Inc.

2 Harris, R. L. (2002). *Exploring the Basics of the Bible* (15). Wheaton, Ill.: Crossway Books.

3 Swindoll, C. R., & Zuck, R. B. (2003). *Understanding Christian Theology* (60). Nashville, Tenn.: Thomas Nelson Publishers.

4 Geisler, N. L., & Brooks, R. M. (1990). *When Skeptics Ask* (144). Wheaton, Ill.: Victor Books.

5 "Christ: The Fulfillment of Prophecy," D. James Kennedy (2007). *The Apologetics Study Bible: Real Questions, Straight Answers, Stronger Faith*. Nashville, TN: Holman Bible Publishers.

6 Harris, R. L. (2002). *Exploring the Basics of the Bible* (20). Wheaton, Ill.: Crossway Books.

7 MacDonald, J. (2002). *God Wrote a Book* (34). Wheaton, Ill.: Crossway Books.

8 McDowell, J. (2006). *Evidence for Christianity* (114). Nashville, TN: Thomas Nelson Publishers.

9 Archer, G. L. (1998). *A Survey of Old Testament Introduction* (3rd. ed.].) (29). Chicago: Moody Press.

10 Ryrie, C. C. (1999). *Basic Theology : A Popular Systematic Guide to Understanding Biblical Truth* (121). Chicago, Ill.: Moody Press.

11 Tan, P. L. (1996). *Encyclopedia of 7700 Illustrations: Signs of the Times*. Garland, TX: Bible Communications, Inc.

12 Cabal, T., Brand, C. O., Clendenen, E. R., Copan, P., Moreland, J., & Powell, D. (2007). *The Apologetics Study Bible: Real Questions, Straight Answers, Stronger Faith* (1148). Nashville, TN: Holman Bible Publishers.

13 MacDonald, J. (2002). *God Wrote a Book* (25). Wheaton, Ill.: Crossway Books.

14 IBID, 26.

15 IBID.

16 McDowell, J. (2006). *Evidence for Christianity* (91). Nashville, TN: Thomas Nelson Publishers.

17 IBID, 131.

18 IBID, 132.

19 Glueck, Nelson (1959). *Rivers in the Desert* (136). New York: Farrar, Strauss and Cudahy.

20 Zacharias, Ravi. (1994). *Can A Man Live Without God?* (162) Nashville, TN: Word.

21 Tan, P. L. (1996). *Encyclopedia of 7700 Illustrations: Signs of the Times*. Garland, TX: Bible Communications, Inc.

22 McDowell, J. (2006). *Evidence for Christianity* (101). Nashville, TN: Thomas Nelson Publishers.

23 Harris, R. L. (2002). *Exploring the Basics of the Bible* (28). Wheaton, Ill.: Crossway Books.

24 LaHaye, T. (2009). *Jesus*. Colorado Springs, CO: David C. Cook.

25 Archer, G. L. (1982). *New International Encyclopedia of Bible Difficulties*. Zondervan's Understand the Bible Reference Series (12). Grand Rapids, MI: Zondervan Publishing House.

26 Tan, P. L. (1996). *Encyclopedia of 7700 Illustrations: Signs of the Times*. Garland, TX: Bible Communications, Inc.

27 Cabal, T., Brand, C. O., Clendenen, E. R., Copan, P., Moreland, J., & Powell, D. (2007). *The Apologetics Study Bible: Real Questions, Straight Answers, Stronger Faith* (468). Nashville, TN: Holman Bible Publishers.

28 Geisler, N. L., & Nix, W. E. (1996). *A General Introduction to the Bible* (Rev. and expanded.) (348–349). Chicago: Moody Press.

29 McDowell, J. (2006). *Evidence for Christianity* (104). Nashville, TN: Thomas Nelson Publishers.

30 IBID, 106.

31 Grudem, W. A. (1994). *Systematic Theology : An Introduction to Biblical Doctrine* (73). Leicester, England; Grand Rapids, Mich.: Inter-Varsity Press; Zondervan Pub. House.

32 Geisler, N. L., & Nix, W. E. (1996). *A General Introduction to the Bible* (Rev. and expanded.) (50–51). Chicago: Moody Press.

33 Grudem, W. A. (1994). *Systematic Theology : An Introduction to Biblical Doctrine* (79). Leicester, England; Grand Rapids, Mich.: Inter-Varsity Press; Zondervan Pub. House.

34 Tan, P. L. (1996). *Encyclopedia of 7700 Illustrations: Signs of the Times*. Garland, TX: Bible Communications, Inc.

35 McDowell, J. (2006). *Evidence for Christianity* (21–25). Nashville, TN: Thomas Nelson Publishers.

36 Geisler, N. L., & Nix, W. E. (1996). *A General Introduction to the Bible* (Rev. and expanded.) (29). Chicago: Moody Press.

37 McDowell, J. (2006). *Evidence for Christianity* (24–25). Nashville, TN: Thomas Nelson Publishers.

38 Swindoll, C. R., & Zuck, R. B. (2003). *Understanding Christian Theology* (47). Nashville, Tenn.: Thomas Nelson Publishers.

39 McDowell, J. (2006). *Evidence for Christianity* (29). Nashville, TN: Thomas Nelson Publishers.

40 Federer, W. J. (2001). *Great Quotations : A Collection of Passages, Phrases, and Quotations Influencing Early and Modern World History Referenced according to their Sources in Literature, Memoirs, Letters, Governmental Documents, Speeches, Charters, Court Decisions and Constitutions*. St. Louis, MO: AmeriSearch.

41 Geisler, N. L., & Nix, W. E. (1996). *A General Introduction to the Bible* (Rev. and expanded.) (196). Chicago: Moody Press.

42 McDowell, J. (2006). *Evidence for Christianity* (34). Nashville, TN: Thomas Nelson Publishers.

43 IBID.

44 Tan, P. L. (1996). *Encyclopedia of 7700 Illustrations: Signs of the Times*. Garland, TX: Bible Communications, Inc.

45 Geisler, N. L., & Turek, F. (2004). *I Don't Have Enough Faith to Be an Atheist* (231). Wheaton, Ill.: Crossway Books.

46 IBID, 276.

47 IBID, 275.

48 Galaxie Software. (2002; 2002). *10,000 Sermon Illustrations*. Biblical Studies Press.

49 Geisler, N. L., & Turek, F. (2004). *I Don't Have Enough Faith to Be an Atheist*

(277–278). Wheaton, Ill.: Crossway Books.
50 IBID, 278.
51 IBID.
52 MacDonald, J. (2002). *God Wrote a Book* (112–113). Wheaton, Ill.: Crossway Books.
53 St. Augustine, Reply to Faustus the Manichaean 11.5 in Philip Schaff, A Select Library of the Nicene and Ante-Nicene Fathers of the Christian Church (Grand Rapids: Eerdmans, 1956), vol. 4.
54 Kotler, P. (2009). *Principles of Marketing.* Indianapolis, IN.: Prentice Hall.
55 Geisler, N. L., & Turek, F. (2004). *I Don't Have Enough Faith to Be an Atheist* (280). Wheaton, Ill.: Crossway Books.
56 Jeremiah, D. (1996). *How to Be Happy According to Jesus: Study Guide* (20). Nashville, Tenn.: Thomas Nelson Publishers.
57 Strobel, L. (1998). *The Case for Christ* (107). Grand Rapids, MI: Zondervan.
58 IBID.
59 Geisler, N. L., & Turek, F. (2004). *I Don't Have Enough Faith to Be an Atheist* (270). Wheaton, Ill.: Crossway Books.
60 McDowell, J. (2006). *Evidence for Christianity* (101). Nashville, TN: Thomas Nelson Publishers.
61 Geisler, N. L., & Brooks, R. M. (1990). *When Skeptics Ask* (203). Wheaton, Ill.: Victor Books.
62 Geisler, N. L., & Turek, F. (2004). *I Don't Have Enough Faith to Be an Atheist* (285). Wheaton, Ill.: Crossway Books.
62 IBID, 286.
64 IBID, 285.
65 Geisler, N. L., & Brooks, R. M. (1990). *When Skeptics Ask* (144). Wheaton, Ill.: Victor Books.
66 MacDonald, J. (2002). *God Wrote a Book* (16–17). Wheaton, Ill.: Crossway Books.
67 Geisler, N. L., & Turek, F. (2004). *I Don't Have Enough Faith to Be an Atheist* (290). Wheaton, Ill.: Crossway Books.
68 IBID.
69 Strobel, L. (1998). *The Case for Christ* (250). Grand Rapids, MI: Zondervan.
70 Geisler, N. L., & Turek, F. (2004). *I Don't Have Enough Faith to Be an Atheist* (292). Wheaton, Ill.: Crossway Books.
71 Charles Colson, "An Unholy Hoax?" Breakpoint Commentary, posted at http://www.breakpoint.org/commentaries/4187-an-unholy-hoax
72 Geisler, N. L., & Turek, F. (2004). *I Don't Have Enough Faith to Be an Atheist* (293). Wheaton, Ill.: Crossway Books.
73 Strobel, L. (1998). *The Case for Christ* (247). Grand Rapids, MI: Zondervan.
74 Swindoll, C. R., & Zuck, R. B. (2003). *Understanding Christian Theology* (155). Nashville, Tenn.: Thomas Nelson Publishers.
75 IBID.
76 IBID.
77 Ryrie, C. C. (1999). *Basic Theology : A Popular Systemic Guide to Understanding Biblical Truth* (54). Chicago, Ill.: Moody Press.
78 Lloyd-Jones, D. M. (1996). *God the Father, God the Son* (79). Wheaton, Ill.: Crossway Books.
79 Ryrie, C. C. (1999). *Basic Theology : A Popular Systematic Guide to Understanding Biblical Truth* (53–54). Chicago, Ill.: Moody Press.

80 Green, M. P. (1989). *Illustrations for Biblical Preaching : Over 1500 Sermon Illustrations Arranged by Topic and Indexed Exhaustively* (Revised edition of: The expositor's illustration file). Grand Rapids: Baker Book House.

81 Ryrie, C. C. (1995). *A Survey of Bible Doctrine.* Chicago: Moody Press.

82 Bickel, B & Jantz, S. (1997). *Bruce & Stan's Guide to God* (68). Eugene, OR: Harvest House.

83 http://dailychristianquote.com/dcqwesleyjohn.html

84 Swindoll, C. R., & Zuck, R. B. (2003). *Understanding Christian Theology* (201). Nashville, Tenn.: Thomas Nelson Publishers.

85 Grudem, W. A. (1994). *Systematic Theology : An Introduction to Biblical Doctrine* (267). Leicester, England; Grand Rapids, Mich.: Inter-Varsity Press; Zondervan Pub. House.

86 Inrig, G. (1981). *Quality Friendship* (52). Chicago, IL: Moody Press.

87 Swindoll, C. R., & Zuck, R. B. (2003). *Understanding Christian Theology* (183). Nashville, Tenn.: Thomas Nelson Publishers.

88 Erickson, M. J. (1998). *Christian Theology* (2nd ed.) (337–338). Grand Rapids, Mich.: Baker Book House.

89 IBID, 344.

90 Lucado, M. (1987). *God Came Near: Chronicles of the Christ* (104–105). Portland, Or.: Multnomah Press.

91 *Tabletalk Magazine: August 1992.* 1992 (5). Lake Mary, FL: Ligonier Ministries, Inc.

92 Swindoll, C. R., & Zuck, R. B. (2003). *Understanding Christian Theology* (150). Nashville, Tenn.: Thomas Nelson Publishers.

93 IBID, 187.

94 Hybels, B. (1997). *The God You're Looking For* (113). Nashville, TN: Thomas Nelson Publishers.

95 Grudem, W. A. (1994). *Systematic Theology : An Introduction to Biblical Doctrine* (197). Leicester, England; Grand Rapids, Mich.: Inter-Varsity Press; Zondervan Pub. House.

96 Barton, B. B. (1993). *John.* Life Application Bible Commentary (210). Wheaton, Ill.: Tyndale House.

97 Geisler, N. L., & Brooks, R. M. (1990). *When Skeptics Ask* (26). Wheaton, Ill.: Victor Books.

98 Lucado, M., & Gibbs, T. A. (2001). *God's Inspirational Promises* (37). Nashville, TN: J. Countryman.

99 Lucado, M., & Gibbs, T. A. (2000). *Grace for the Moment: Inspirational Thoughts for Each Day of the Year* (285). Nashville, Tenn.: J. Countryman.

100 Tozer, A. W., & Fessenden, D. E. (2001-). *The Attributes of God,* Volume 2: Deeper Into the Father's Heart (84). Camp Hill, PA: WingSpread.

101 Packer, J. I. (1995). *Concise theology: A Guide to Historic Christian Beliefs.* Wheaton, Ill.: Tyndale House.

102 Chambers, O. (1996). *Biblical Ethics.* Hants UK: Marshall, Morgan & Scott.

103 Tozer, A. W., & Eggert, R. (1998). *Vol. 1: The Tozer Topical Reader* (296). Camp Hill, PA.: WingSpread.

104 Merriam-Webster, I. (1992). *The Merriam-Webster Dictionary of Quotations.* (334). Springfield, Mass.: Merriam-Webster.

105 Streiker, L. D. (2000). *Nelson's Big Book of Laughter: Thousands of Smiles from A to Z* (electronic ed.) (348). Nashville: Thomas Nelson Publishers.

106 Morgan, R. J. (2000). *Nelson's Complete Book of Stories, Illustrations, and Quotes* (electronic ed.) (148). Nashville: Thomas Nelson Publishers.

107 Federer, W. J. (2001). *Great Quotations : A Collection of Passages, Phrases, and Quotations Influencing Early and Modern World History Referenced according to their Sources in Literature, Memoirs, Letters, Governmental Documents, Speeches, Charters, Court Decisions and Constitutions*. St. Louis, MO: AmeriSearch.

108 Osbeck, K. W. (1982). *101 Hymn Stories*. Grand Rapids, Mich.: Kregel Publications.

109 Richards, L. (1990). *The 365 Day Devotional Commentary* (317). Wheaton, IL: Victor Books.

110 Walvoord, J. F., Zuck, R. B., & Dallas Theological Seminary. (1983-). Vol. 1: *The Bible Knowledge Commentary: An Exposition of the Scriptures* (1507). Wheaton, IL: Victor Books.

111 Richards, L. (1990). *The 365 Day Devotional Commentary* (317). Wheaton, IL: Victor Books.

112 Richards, L. (1990). *The 365 Day Devotional Commentary* (639). Wheaton, IL: Victor Books.

113 Chambers, O. (1996). *Not Knowing Where*. Grand Rapids: Discovery House.

114 Swindoll, C. R., & Zuck, R. B. (2003). *Understanding Christian Theology* (235). Nashville, Tenn.: Thomas Nelson Publishers.

115 Zodhiates, S. (1999). *Faith, Love, & Hope: An Exposition of the Epistle of James* (electronic ed.). Logos Library System; Exegetical Commentary Series (Jas 2:23). Chattanooga, TN: AMG Publishers.

116 Grudem, W. A. (1994). *Systematic Theology: An Introduction to Biblical Doctrine* (205). Leicester, England; Grand Rapids, Mich.: Inter-Varsity Press; Zondervan Pub. House.

117 Ryken, P. G., & Hughes, R. K. (2005). *Exodus: Saved for God's Glory* (1056). Wheaton, Ill.: Crossway Books.

118 Geisler, N. L. (2003). *Systematic Theology, Volume Two: God, Creation* (339–340). Minneapolis, MN: Bethany House Publishers.

119 Barton, B. B. (1993). *John*. Life application Bible commentary (188–189). Wheaton, Ill.: Tyndale House.

120 Anders, M. E. (1999). *New Christian's Handbook: Everything New Believers Need to Know: What to Believe, Why We Believe It, How We Live It* (210). Nashville, Tenn.: T. Nelson Publishers.

121 Grudem, W. A. (1994). *Systematic Theology: An Introduction to Biblical Doctrine* (553–554). Leicester, England; Grand Rapids, Mich.: Inter-Varsity Press; Zondervan Pub. House.

122 Anders, M. E. (1999). *New Christian's Handbook: Everything New Believers Need to Know: What to Believe, Why We Believe It, How We Live It* (216). Nashville, Tenn.: T. Nelson Publishers.

123 Paul Westervelt, P. (2005; 2006). *Discipleship Journal*, Issue 148 (July/August 2005). NavPress.

124 Paul Westervelt, P. (2005; 2006). *Discipleship Journal*, Issue 148 (July/August 2005). NavPress.

125 Geisler, N. L., & Brooks, R. M. (1990). *When Skeptics Ask* (103–104). Wheaton, Ill.: Victor Books.

126 Paul Westervelt, P. (2005; 2006). *Discipleship Journal*, Issue 148 (July/August 2005). NavPress.

127 MacDonald, W., & Farstad, A. (1997). *Believer's Bible Commentary: Old and New Testaments* (Ps 103:3). Nashville: Thomas Nelson.

128 Geddert, T. J. (2001). *Mark*. Believers Church Bible Commentary (297). Scottdale, Pa.: Herald Press.

129 Merriam-Webster, I. (1992). *The Merriam-Webster Dictionary of Quotations.* (210). Springfield, Mass.: Merriam-Webster.

130 Lucado, M. (2003). *Next Door Savior* (106). Nashville, Tenn.: W Pub. Group.

131 Swindoll, C. R., & Zuck, R. B. (2003). *Understanding Christian Theology* (799). Nashville, Tenn.: Thomas Nelson Publishers.

132 Paul Westervelt, P. (2005; 2006). *Discipleship Journal,* Issue 148 (July/August 2005). NavPress.

133 Cabal, T., Brand, C. O., Clendenen, E. R., Copan, P., Moreland, J., & Powell, D. (2007). *The Apologetics Study Bible: Real Questions, Straight Answers, Stronger Faith* (1826). Nashville, TN: Holman Bible Publishers.

134 *AMG Bible Illustrations.* 2000. Bible Illustrations Series. Chattanooga: AMG Publishers.

135 Kaiser, W. C., Jr., Davids, P. H., Bruce, F. F., & Brauch, M. T. (1997). *Hard Sayings of the Bible* (500). Downers Grove, Il: InterVarsity.

136 I heard author and speaker Strobel speak at Saddleback Church, approx. 2001. Strobel, a former journalist, is the author of a series of *The Case for* books, including his positing the case for Christ, Easter, and other topics.

137 Chapell, B., Carson, D. A., & Keller, T. (2011). *What Is the Gospel?*. Wheaton, IL: Crossway.

138 Kaiser, W. C., Jr., Davids, P. H., Bruce, F. F., & Brauch, M. T. (1997). *Hard Sayings of the Bible* (502). Downers Grove, Il: InterVarsity.

139 *Time,* June 4, 1979.

140 McDowell, J. (2006). *Evidence for Christianity* (318). Nashville, TN: Thomas Nelson Publishers.

141 IBID, 323.

142 IBID, 324.

143 IBID, 335.

144 IBID, 349.

145 Larson, C. B., & Lowery, B. (2009). *1001 Quotations That Connect: Timeless Wisdom for Preaching, Teaching, and Writing* (222). Grand Rapids, MI: Zondervan Publishing House.

146 McDowell, J. (2006). *Evidence for Christianity* (244–245). Nashville, TN: Thomas Nelson Publishers.

147 Wright, N. T. (1994). *Following Jesus: Biblical Reflections on Discipleship* (60). London: Society for Promoting Christian Knowledge.

148 Larson, C. B., & Lowery, B. (2009). *1001 Quotations That Connect: Timeless Wisdom for Preaching, Teaching, and Writing* (301). Grand Rapids, MI: Zondervan Publishing House.

149 Smith, C. S. (2002). *Unlocking the Bible Story,* Volume 1 (100). Chicago, IL: Moody Press.

150 Radmacher, E. D., Allen, R. B., & House, H. W. (1999). *Nelson's New Illustrated Bible Commentary* (Ro 3:24). Nashville: T. Nelson Publishers.

151 Barton, B. B., Veerman, D., Taylor, L. C., & Comfort, P. W. (1997). Hebrews. *Life Application Bible Commentary* (157). Wheaton, Ill.: Tyndale House Publishers.

152 Paul Westervelt, P. (1994; 2006). *Discipleship Journal,* Issue 82 (July/August 1994). NavPress.

153 Barton, B. B. (1993). *John*. Life Application Bible Commentary (62). Wheaton, Ill.: Tyndale House.

154 Carson, D. A. (2000). *The Difficult Doctrine of the Love of God* (63). Wheaton, Ill.: Crossway Books.

155 Piper, J. (2006). *Fifty Reasons Why Jesus Came to Die* (28). Wheaton, Ill.: Crossway Books.

156 Barton, B. B. (1993). *John*. Life Application Bible Commentary (64). Wheaton, Ill.: Tyndale House.

157 For more on Dave Roever's story and ministry, visit http://daveroever.org/ roeverstory.php.

158 Richards, L. (1990). *The 365 Day Devotional Commentary* (1047). Wheaton, IL: Victor Books.

159 Larson, C. B., & Lowery, B. (2009). *1001 Quotations That Connect: Timeless Wisdom for Preaching, Teaching, and Writing* (183). Grand Rapids, MI: Zondervan Publishing House.

160 Piper, John. (2004). *The Passion of Jesus Christ* (34). Wheaton, IL: Crossway Books.

161 Lloyd-Jones, D. M. (2000). *Authentic Christianity* (1st U.S. ed.) (197). Wheaton, Ill.: Crossway Books.

162 Vander Meulen, E. L. (2005). *His Names are Wonderful: Getting to Know God Through His Hebrew Names* (50). Baltimore, MD: Lederer Books.

163 Adapted from "Arise, Sir Knight," a sermon by James Allan Francis, in *The Real Jesus and Other Sermons* (Philadelphia: Judson, 1926), 123–124.

164 *Emmaus Journal, Volume 10.* 2001 (1) (151). Dubuque, IA: Emmaus Bible College.

165 Larson, C. B., & Lowery, B. (2009). *1001 Quotations That Connect: Timeless Wisdom for Preaching, Teaching, and Writing* (301). Grand Rapids, MI: Zondervan Publishing House.

166 Torrey, R. A., Feinberg, C. L., & Wiersbe, W. W. Vol. 3: *The Fundamentals: The Famous Sourcebook of Foundational Biblical Truths* (364). Public Domain.

167 Anders, M. E. (1999). *New Christian's Handbook: Everything New Believers Need to Know: What to Believe, Why We Believe It, How We Live It* (53). Nashville, Tenn.: T. Nelson Publishers.

168 Erickson, M. J. (1998). *Christian Theology* (2nd ed.) (879). Grand Rapids, Mich.: Baker Book House.

169 Larson, C. B., & Lowery, B. (2009). *1001 Quotations That Connect: Timeless Wisdom for Preaching, Teaching, and Writing* (173). Grand Rapids, MI: Zondervan Publishing House.

170 Barton, B. B., Veerman, D., & Wilson, N. S. (1992). *Romans.* Life Application Bible Commentary (152). Wheaton, IL: Tyndale House Publishers.

171 Wiersbe, W. W. (1997). *With the Word Bible Commentary* (Eph 5:1). Nashville: Thomas Nelson.

172 Swindoll, C. R., & Zuck, R. B. (2003). *Understanding Christian Theology* (499). Nashville, Tenn.: Thomas Nelson Publishers.

173 Tozer, A. W. (2007). *God's Pursuit of Man* (100). Camp Hill, PA: WingSpread.

174 Larson, C. B., & Lowery, B. (2009). *1001 Quotations That Connect: Timeless Wisdom for Preaching, Teaching, and Writing* (279). Grand Rapids, MI: Zondervan Publishing House.

175 Tozer, A. W. (1993). *The Counselor: Straight Talk about the Holy Spirit from a 20th Century Prophet* (71). Camp Hill, PA.: WingSpread.

176 Larson, C. B., & Ten Elshof, P. (2008). *1001 Illustrations That Connect* (317). Grand Rapids, MI: Zondervan Publishing House.

177 IBID, 283.

178 Ryrie, C. C. (1999). *Basic Theology: A Popular Systematic Guide to Understanding Biblical Truth* (416). Chicago, Ill.: Moody Press.

179 Morgan, R. J. (2007). *Nelson's Annual Preacher's Sourcebook: 2008 Edition* (305). Nashville, TN: Thomas Nelson Publishers.

180 IBID, 19.

181 Tozer, A. W., & Smith, G. B. (1991). *Renewed Day by Day: A Daily Devotional.* Camp Hill, PA.: WingSpread.

182 Lucado, M. (1994). *When God Whispers Your Name* (37). Dallas: Word Pub.

52 WAYS TO GROW YOUR FAITH will do what it says AND give you freedom. Your spiritual growth strategy does not have to be limited to reading and praying. Try growing spiritually while walking, driving, or working out. 52 *Ways to Grow Your Faith* will jump-start a stalled faith, provide a road map for a new faith, or simply energize an active faith. Use this resource with friends in a weekly study group or on your own — but get ready to grow and connect with God in a busy, noisy world.

EACH CHAPTER INCLUDES
• Spiritual growth idea and explanation
• Key verse (the Bible's connection)
• Devotion (life's connection)
• Quote (sometimes humorous, always thoughtful)
• Try It (tip for application)
• I Tried It! (real people, real stories)
• Prayer

THE 52 SERIES

BY GREGG PETER FARAH

AVAILABLE NOW!
52 Reasons to Believe
Concise Thoughts on the Christian Faith

AVAILABLE NOW!
52 Ways to Grow Your Faith
Connect with God in a Busy, Noisy World

COMING SOON!
52 Reasons to Question Your Faith
Questions That Need Answers

COMING SOON!
52 Bible Verses That'll Change Your Life
If You Only Know ONE Verse, Know This One . . .

For more information, to receive email updates, or to place an order, visit gpfarah.com/52series or phone 646-335-3342.